Famous scientists and inventors

Also available from Questions Publishing Company Ltd

Famous Mathematicians
John Davis

ISBN: 1-84190-028-1

Famous scientists and inventors

Learning from the lives of key thinkers

Activities for Key Stage 2

John Davis

QUESTIONS PUBLISHING

27 Frederick Street, Birmingham B1 3HH

First published in 2000 by
The Questions Publishing Company Ltd
27 Frederick Street, Birmingham B1 3HH

Designed and typeset by Keystroke, Jacaranda House, Wolverhampton
Edited by Margaret Deith
Illustrations by Jane Bottomley and Peter Wilks
Cover design by James Davies

ISBN: 1-84190-037-0

With grateful thanks to the children and staff of Warmley Primary School,
South Gloucestershire, for all their patience and assistance.

Contents

Introduction

Which Victorian engineer and inventor started designing bridges while recovering from an accident? Who grew over 30,000 versions of the same plant so that he could study their characteristics? Who was locked up in his house for the last ten years of his life because of what he wrote? Who got sent down from university because of an outbreak of the plague?

The answers to these questions and more are provided in *Famous Scientists and Inventors* as it looks at some of the key figures that have shaped science as we know it, and who remain influential in primary school science today.

Each chapter opens with biographical information about the chosen individual, putting each into his or her historical setting. This section has been written for children to read for themselves, and is intended, once copied, to be suitable for use as a piece of factual information during the text-level part of the Literacy Hour.

Details then follow of how each of our key thinkers' work relates to Key Stage 2 science teaching today, and a range of differentiated practical classroom-based tasks are provided for children to carry out. The activities outlined, featuring a variety of largely 'hands-on' experiments and investigations, are aimed at helping to boost teachers' confidence in the delivery of the science curriculum. They involve the use of resources, equipment and materials that are easy to collect, assemble and organise. Tasks are set in a variety of domestic and environmental contexts that all children will be familiar with. They also seek to illustrate to the children the part played by science and technology in the development of useful things. The book is not intended to be a science scheme of work, but to provide valuable yet manageable tasks that can be adapted for use in primary schools.

Suggestions are given at the end of each chapter about how to support lower-ability children, and there are also ideas about extension work for those in the higher-ability range. Because language is such a crucial aspect of science teaching, a word bank of essential vocabulary is included along with a list of necessary resources. Each chapter contains two photocopiable tasks related to some aspect of the activities described. All practical work is cross-referenced to both the science and design and technology sections of the Curriculum 2000 document because of the close relationship between the two areas. Science One: Scientific Enquiry is listed for each chapter in view of its vital importance in teaching the subject. Work has also been closely linked to the DfEE/QCA publication, *Science: A Scheme of Work for Key Stages 1 and 2*. Short suggestions are made at the end of each chapter about the part that can be played by ICT.

Health and safety note: Brief mention is made in some chapters of important health and safety procedures when practical work is being carried out, but these are not described in detail. It is essential that all teachers, support staff and helpers involved in primary school science and design and technology teaching are fully conversant with all school and local authority rules that apply to these areas of the curriculum, and ensure that they are always carried out.

1
Isambard Kingdom Brunel
Speeding up travel

Some people never emerge from beneath the shadow of a famous parent. Unkind comparisons are often made regarding achievements, and many find it difficult to establish a reputation of their own.

This was certainly not true of Isambard Kingdom Brunel. He wisely used the knowledge and experience he gained from working with his father in his early years to develop his own style and expertise as one of the foremost designers, engineers and technologists of the Victorian era. His work touched the lives of countless people and in many places changed the landscape for ever.

Marc Brunel, Isambard's father, came from France. He fled to New York to escape the worst excesses of the French Revolution but eventually settled in England. Isambard, who was born in Portsmouth in 1806, had an English mother and it was from her that he adopted the name Kingdom – her surname before she was married.

As an engineer, Marc Brunel is best known for the difficult, but eventually successful, construction of the first tunnel under the River Thames in London. The tunnel, that stretched from Rotherhithe to Wapping, took eighteen years to complete and required the design and construction of a special machine called a tunnelling shield, which not only moved the tunnel forward but also prevented its collapse until the hole could be lined. It was an ill-fated project. Work often stopped for long periods because of money problems, and flooding caused several major accidents. In one incident Isambard was almost killed and it was while he was recuperating from his injuries that his own career began to take off.

Some of his recovery time was spent in Bristol, and it was here in 1828 that Brunel junior decided to enter a competition to design a bridge to span the Avon Gorge at Clifton. Brunel's design, in a modified form, was finally accepted despite fierce competition from famous engineers like Thomas Telford. But financial problems held up the building of the bridge and it was not completed until after Brunel's death in 1859.

After carrying out further engineering work to improve the docks in the centre of Bristol, Brunel was appointed chief engineer of the Great Western Railway in 1833. During his lifetime he was responsible for the laying of over 1,000 miles (1,600 kilometres) of railway track throughout Britain and Ireland, as well as the bridges to carry the lines over rivers and roads and the tunnels to take them through hillsides. The bridges at Chepstow and Saltash are among his best-known memorials, while the two-mile long Box Tunnel on the Bristol to London line took five years to dig. When the two tunnels being made from either side finally met in the middle, they were only three centimetres out, even though the tunnel had been built with a deliberate bend in it.

While his railways were opening up the country for millions of people and stimulating trade and industry, Brunel was simultaneously working hard to design and build ships that would transport travellers around the world faster and more safely. The three main ships with which he is associated, the *Great Western*, the *Great Britain* and the *Great Eastern*, were built between 1838 and 1858 and were all at the leading edge of design and construction. The paddle steamer *Great Western* crossed the Atlantic Ocean in only fifteen days; the *Great Britain* was the first propeller-driven ocean-going steamship; and the *Great Eastern*, with its hull made from a double skin of iron, could carry up to 4,000 passengers. All were the largest ships of their kind when they were launched, and incorporated the very latest technology.

By 1859 Brunel, who took few holidays, often slept in his office and went for long spells without eating, was suffering from poor health. Years of master-minding complex tasks, having to deal with management squabbles and raising the necessary funding from private investors had taken their toll. While watching sea trials of the *Great Eastern* he had a stroke and ten days later he died at the age of only fifty-three.

BRIDGING THE GAP

Although their uses may vary greatly, all bridges stem from the same basic designs. Introducing children to these designs will not only help them to construct their own simple bridges, but also increase their understanding of how successfully bridges do their job when they are put under strain. Use videos, books, magazines, posters and photographs to show children the most common types of bridge, especially beam, arch, cantilever and suspension. Consider each example of a bridge in its context and environment.

- What materials have been used to build it?
- How have these materials been used?
- What does the bridge span?
- What and who would need to use the bridge?

Begin with some practical focused tasks using a simple beam bridge across two pillars (see Figure 1.1). Fold lengths of card to make differently-shaped girders and then test their strength with coins or small weights. Possible shapes for the test girders are shown in Figure 1.2. Does folding and bending the girders make them stronger? Stress the importance of keeping the test fair by using the same length and type of card and the same gap between the pillars each time.

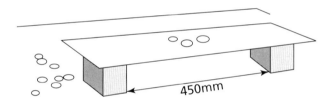

● Figure 1.1: Simple beam bridge

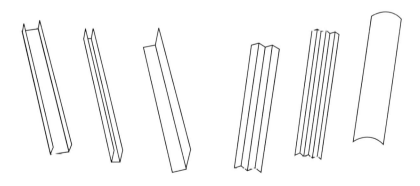

● Figure 1.2: Possible shapes for test girders

Next try some arch designs. Some possibilities are shown in Figure 1.3. Ask the children to try different spans and again test with weights.

- How does changing the span alter the strength of the arch?
- What happens if the span is kept constant but the height of the arch varied?

Different lengths of card will be needed in order to do this.

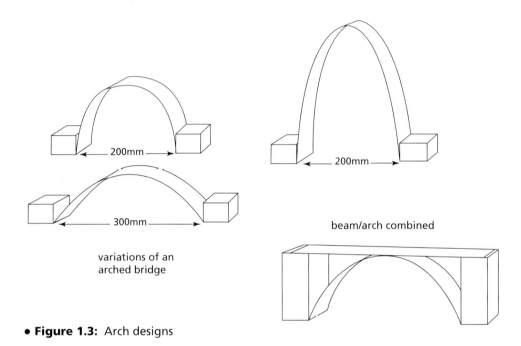

variations of an
arched bridge

beam/arch combined

• **Figure 1.3:** Arch designs

Think about the forces on an arch and the important part played by the keystone (see Figure 1.4). Does using a beam and an arch together make a stronger bridge?

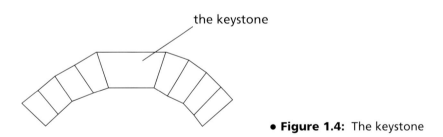

the keystone

• **Figure 1.4:** The keystone

Cantilever bridges, commonly seen on motorways, consist of a long beam resting on brackets at each end. These are called cantilevers. If the same loads are put at A and B, what is the greatest load that can be put at the centre? (See Figure 1.5.) Children will soon discover that as the central load is increased so the loads at A and B will also need to be added to. Ask them to test for the viable length of the central span while keeping the lengths of the side pieces constant, and then vary the length of the side pieces while the length of the central span remains unchanged.

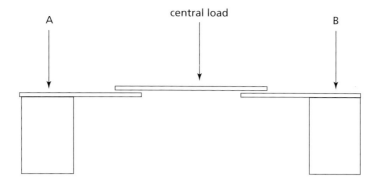

● **Figure 1.5:** Cantilever bridge

Finally, before the children turn their practical testing and evaluations into designs and models of their own bridges, work on a large scale by making a class suspension bridge. Use a range of different materials including chairs, string, bricks and a short, light plank for the decking (see Figure 1.6). Encourage children to think about its construction.

● Why must the chairs be positioned correctly?
● Why is the use of the bricks so important?
● What materials would replace the string in normal sized bridges?
● Why are suspension bridges like this often closed during periods of bad weather?

These days designers, engineers and builders have the latest materials, technology and equipment at their disposal. But how is bridge building carried out in remote areas where only materials that are found naturally in the environment are available to use? Pose this kind of construction challenge for the children by using the photo-copiable sheet *Crossing the ravine*.

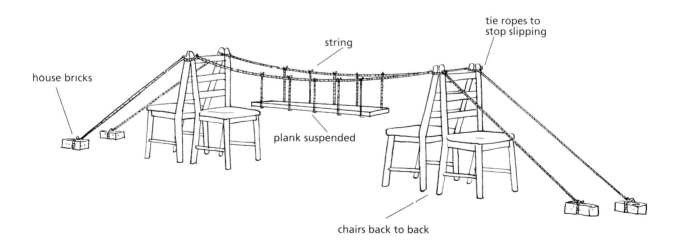

● **Figure 1.6:** Class-made suspension bridge

Tunnelling away

Tunnels are built under water, under land or through hills and mountains to take road and rail traffic. The earth, rock or water above them exerts a very large force. Designers and engineers always have to take this important fact into consideration and maximum strength is always a prime concern. Discuss the different kinds of tunnels that the children might have used, especially the one under the English Channel that joins England and France. This has proved to be extremely successful and already plans are being discussed to construct a second underwater link between the two countries.

Investigate the best shape for a tunnel. Start with some tubes about 20 cm long and 10 cm in diameter made out of different types of card. Bury them in sand but leave one of the ends open to enable good observation of what happens to them (see Figure 1.7). Also try square, rectangular and triangular shapes. Pile up the same amounts of sand on top and keep tunnels the same length and height to make the test as fair as possible.

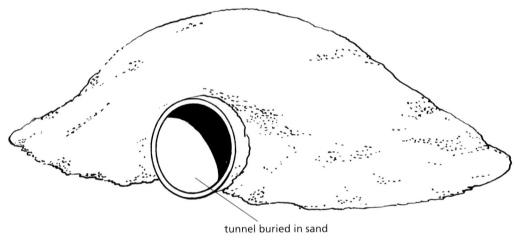

tunnel buried in sand

● **Figure 1.7:** Testing tunnels

● Which shape of tunnel has been able to withstand the greatest pressure from above?
● Are there points in the tunnel where engineers would need to think about strengthening their design?

This should lead to the children suggesting that pillars are often used to support heavy loads in tunnels. Make some pillars with different cross-sections and compare the loads they are able to take before collapse when they are tested with weights (see Figure 1.8). Try tubes of different diameters first. Does the type of paper or card they are made of make a difference? Then experiment with other shapes. Try different heights with the same shape. Encourage the children to consider the qualities of a good pillar.

● Is a short fat pillar, for example, better than a tall thin one?
● Is the position of pillars in a tunnel important?
● What factors determine how many are needed?

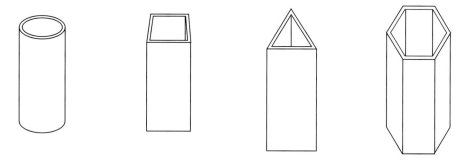

● **Figure 1.8:** Pillar shapes for testing

All at sea

One of the major questions facing Brunel during the design and construction of his large ocean-going ships like the *Great Britain* was how well these large objects would float and move through the water under power.

Using information books and other reference materials, gather together a collection of pictures of ships, boats and other water craft showing a range of different hull shapes. It may also be possible to stimulate further observation and discussion by mounting a display of model boats in the classroom.

Divide the class into small groups of three or four. Provide each group with a large sheet of paper and pencils and encourage them to design three or four different hull shapes, which are approximately the same size but have different features. Some possibilities are shown in Figure 1.9. Once the children are happy with their designs, use tracing paper to transfer the designs to balsa or other types of thin wood. The shapes should then be cut out carefully with a saw and any rough edges smoothed with sandpaper. When the models are ready they should be placed in a suitable water tank. Gentle hand propulsion should then be used to see how well they move and

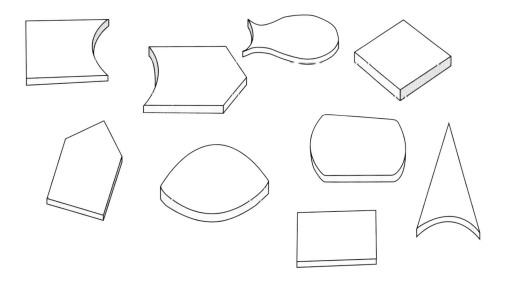

Figure 1.9: Hull shapes

how buoyant they are. One of the easiest ways of making a water tank for use in the classroom is to cut a section of plastic drainpipe about two metres long and mount it on wooden blocks. This will provide a narrow channel that helps to keep the proto-type hulls moving along a straight course (see Figure 1.10).

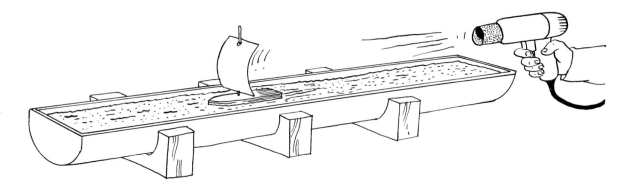

● **Figure 1.10:** Channel water tank

There are a number of ways in which this activity can be developed. Ask the children, for example, to construct boats with more built-up hull shapes and then experiment with different materials and methods of waterproofing. Try materials like wood, plastic, metal and cardboard and coverings like pastel crayon, wax crayon and oil- and water-based paints. Which works best? Consider improving the stability by splitting the hull into two parts like a catamaran, or try making hulls from plastic bottles to see whether they are more stable than the ones made from other materials. Further experimentation work on stability is given on the photocopiable sheet *Boat building*.

SUPPORT

It may be necessary to have pre-cut strips of card ready for the children to use for their prototype bridges especially if accurate measurements are needed. Help with other folding, shaping and fixing work. Assistance and support will be needed when testing is being carried out. Simplify data-collection sheets when results of practical work are being recorded. This advice also applies to the tasks involving tunnels. When hull shapes are being drawn and cut out, provide simple templates for the children to use. Close supervision will also be needed when saws are being used to cut the shapes out.

EXTENSION

During the bridge-building activities, children may be able to design and make bridges that have a number of moving parts. Encourage them initially to think about drawbridges and how they might be lifted and lowered to permit entry. Then move on to more complex examples like Tower Bridge, with a pair of arms that have to be raised to allow shipping to pass underneath, and swing bridges that pivot from a fixed point. When children are building boats, ask them to consider other methods of propulsion than moving with the hand or using wind. Tell them to experiment with elastic bands, for example, to work some form of propeller or paddle system at the rear of the boat that can be used to drive it forward.

KEY VOCABULARY

Span, beam bridge, arch bridge, keystone, cantilever bridge, suspension bridge, swing bridge, pillar, girder, constant, central, force, pressure, tube, cross-section, rectangular, triangular, hull, waterproof, catamaran, stability, prototype, propeller, paddle.

RESOURCES

Pictures of bridges, cardboard of different thickness, coins and small weights for testing, scissors, pencils, paper fasteners, sticky tape, glue, string, several house bricks, classroom chairs, small light wooden plank, sand, sand tray, offcuts of thin wood like balsa, saws, sandpaper, rulers, A3 paper, tracing paper, information books showing various types of water transport, model boats, water tank for testing purposes, the photocopiable sheets *Crossing the ravine* and *Boat building*.

NATIONAL CURRICULUM LINKS

Key Stage 2 Science

- Sc 1 Scientific enquiry: 1 Ideas and evidence in science. 2 Investigative skills.
- Sc 3 Materials and their properties: 1 grouping and classifying materials – pupils should be taught to (a) compare everyday materials and objects on the basis of their material properties including hardness, strength, flexibility.
- Sc 4 Physical processes: 2 Forces and motion – pupils should be taught (e) how to measure forces and identify the direction in which they act.

Key Stage 2 Design and technology

- 1 Developing, planning and communicating ideas.
- 2 Working with tools, equipment, materials and components to make quality products.
- 3 Evaluating processes and products.
- 4 Knowledge and understanding of materials and components: pupils should be taught (a) how the working characteristics of materials affect the ways they are used; (b) how materials are combined and mixed to create useful properties.
- 5 Breadth of study: during the key stage, pupils should be taught the knowledge, skills and understanding through (a) investigating and evaluating familiar products, thinking about how they work and how they are used.

ICT suggestions

Word processing for reports of investigations; use of computer for control technology; making models with moving parts.

You are on an expedition when you come to this ravine. There is no way round. Design and then make a suitable bridge to cross the ravine. Try to use as many natural materials as you can, e.g. wood, grass, stone. Draw your plan on the sheet and then make notes about what you need to do.

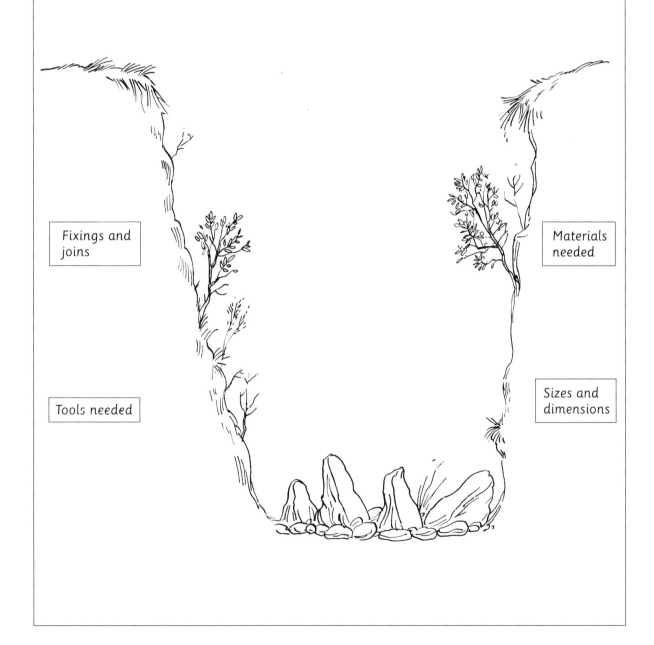

Fixings and joins

Materials needed

Tools needed

Sizes and dimensions

Design and build a sailing craft of some kind.
- It will be powered by a hair dryer blowing a sail.
- It will need to be stable enough to carry cargo and will be tested with small weights.
- Think about ways in which it can be made completely waterproof.

Use this sheet for your planning and draw a sketch of what your sailing craft will look like.

Shape of hull	
Size of hull (l,b)	
Shape of sail	
Size of sail	
Waterproofing	
Position of cargo	

Sketch:

2
Sir Isaac Newton
Letting in the light

It is a strange twist of fate that some of the most important discoveries ever made in the history of science probably happened because of a sudden and dramatic outbreak of one of the world's most dangerous diseases.

When the plague struck in England in 1665, many colleges and universities were closed to prevent the epidemic spreading further. As a result, Isaac Newton, then twenty-two years old, returned to his family home in rural Lincolnshire. Here, free to spend the hours thinking and experimenting in peace and solitude, he was able to formulate his scientific theories on light and gravity as well as study mathematics and astronomy.

Newton was a sickly child. He was born prematurely on Christmas Day in 1643 and, when the midwife left soon after his birth to fetch some important medicine for him, she did not expect him to be alive when she returned. But survive he did and, after his widowed mother remarried and moved to a nearby village, he was left, at the age of only four, in the care of his grandmother. After an early education in the country, he moved to the grammar school in the nearby town of Grantham, where he showed little promise. He spent much of his spare time making working models, including sundials, windmills and kites, and all his pocket money went to buy tools so that he could construct better gadgets. Teachers described him as 'idle' and 'inattentive' and it was only through the influence of an uncle that he was able to go to Trinity College, Cambridge, in 1661.

At Cambridge, Newton met and worked with the man who was to have the greatest influence on his life, Isaac Barrow, professor of mathematics. He encouraged Newton to think for himself and, following the two years spent at home because of the plague, Newton took over Barrow's position when his mentor retired in 1669. Newton became a Fellow of the important scientific organisation the Royal Society in 1672 following his work on a reflecting telescope. Fifteen years later he published *Principia*, often regarded as the greatest science book ever written. In later life, Newton's health was not good and he retired from research work in 1693. He became first Warden and then Master of the Royal Mint in London and was elected President of the Royal Society. Knighted by Queen Anne in 1708, Newton died in 1727 and is buried in Westminster Abbey.

Newton's scientific achievements were massive. His experiments on passing white light through a prism to produce a spectrum of colours led to further investigations into the nature of light and optics. His work on gravity and the laws of motion is also legendary. He discovered one of the fundamental rules of science, which states that for every action there is an equal reaction.

In mathematics, working independently from other mathematicians of the time like Leibniz (see *Famous Mathematicians*, the companion volume to this one), he laid the foundations for calculus, a branch of mathematics that aims to establish rules about the way in which things change or measures quantities by dividing them up into small parts. Newton also showed that comets were objects acted upon by the same forces as planets, and put forward the idea that artificial satellites could be put into orbit around the Earth 300 years before Sputnik was launched and technology finally caught up with his imagination. Newton was the first person to attribute the tides of the sea to the gravitational pull of the Moon on the Earth, and found out that the tides were always bigger when the Sun and Moon were in line with each other and pulled together. Even in retirement at the Royal Mint he continued to work and is said to have sent many forgers to the gallows because of the expert way in which he detected counterfeit money.

Newton was a complex character. He acknowledged his debt to other scientists by modestly admitting: 'If I have seen further, it is by standing on the shoulders of giants.' Yet he also had a fierce temper and delayed publishing many of his discoveries until after the death of any rivals who he thought might turn out to be critical. Despite long nights without sleep while he was observing the stars and planets and days spent writing that often made him unwell, he was eighty-five years old when he died.

RAINBOW COLOURS

Without light, no form of life would be possible. We not only need light to see by but light from the Sun is practically the only source of all our heat and energy. Challenge the children to list or draw as many different sources of light as possible. Encourage them to extend the range from the primitive flame of a candle to the flashing and rotating multicoloured bulbs of a sophisticated disco lighting system. Talk about how the sources vary. Some, like the candle flame and light bulb, get very hot. Others, like fluorescent tubes, only get warm while the glowing digital display on a clock radio, made by the LED or Light Emitting Diode, always remains cold.

Help children to understand that light has to enter our eyes from objects in order for us to see them. Explain that the eye actually sees things upside-down, that the optic nerve carries information about what we see to the brain and that, after information has been taken in by the brain, images are turned the right way up. Make a careful but close examination of the eyes.

- Why does the pupil size change?
- How does it do this?
- What is the coloured part of the eye called?
- What job does the retina do?
- Why do we need to blink?
- Where do tears come from?
- Why do some people need to wear glasses?

Remind children that, as useful as our eyes can be, they can at times play tricks on us. These situations are optical illusions and some interesting examples to investigate are shown on the photocopiable sheet *Optical illusions*.

It was in 1666, while Newton was away from Cambridge University escaping from the plague, that he first realised that, although in normal circumstances light appears to be white, it is in fact made up of a spectrum of colours. He allowed a shaft of light into his darkened room through a tiny hole in his window shutters. After it had passed through a glass prism he had specially cut, the spectrum could be observed on the wall opposite. Later in 1704 he wrote about it in his book *Opticks*. Talk about the mnemonic Richard Of York Gave Battle In Vain to help children remember the order of the spectrum colours, although they may be able to suggest more up-to-date alternatives.

Figure 2.1 shows one way of producing the spectrum effect in the classroom but encourage children to think about other situations that might have the same result. Talk about how a rainbow is produced in the sky when sunlight shines through millions of water droplets. Or observe rainbow colours as bubbles are blown through a wire frame. Look for the spectrum through a glass jar of water placed on a sunny windowsill. Outside, hold a hose pipe so that the water falls in an arch. Stand between the arch and the sun and look where the light shines through the falling droplets.

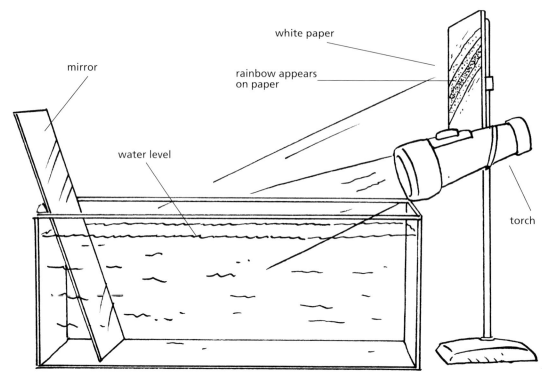

white paper

mirror

rainbow appears
on paper

water level

torch

Hold torch near the dish. Shine light on part of the mirror
under the water

● **Figure 2.1:** The spectrum effect

A shadowy affair

When light from a source hits an object it passes right through, bounces off or becomes absorbed like water being soaked up by a paper tissue. Some materials, like glass and clear plastic, that let light through are called transparent. Others allow some light to pass through but present no clear image. These are described as being translucent. Substances that block the passage of light are said to be opaque; when light hits an object of this kind a shadow is cast. Ask children to test a wide range of materials and to arrange them into each of the three categories. Try collections of various papers and fabrics. Look at different kinds of glass and plastic. Record the findings in chart form (Figure 2.2). Discover whether it is possible to change the way in which materials let light pass through. Paper is usually opaque, but if it is rubbed with oil can it be made translucent? Clear plastic or perspex is transparent, but what happens if the surface is rubbed with sandpaper?

Also carry out simple activities to show that, because light travels in straight lines and cannot bend around objects, shadows are the same shape as the objects themselves. Investigate what happens to the shadow when the opaque object is moved closer to the light source and then further away.

● Are there degrees of darkness visible within the shadows themselves?
● Can the children explain why this phenomenon might occur?

material	transparent	opaque	translucent
1			
2			
3			
4			

Tick the correct box

• **Figure 2.2:** Recording the findings

Extend children's understanding of shadows and how they are formed by setting up other activities both inside and outside the classroom. Make profile silhouettes of the children by sitting them between a desk lamp or a projector and a large sheet of white paper pinned on the wall. Draw around the outline of the shadow. Can the children recognise each other from their silhouettes (Figure 2.3)? Construct some shadow puppets from card and attach them to rods. Stories from different countries and cultures are often performed in this way (Figure 2.4).

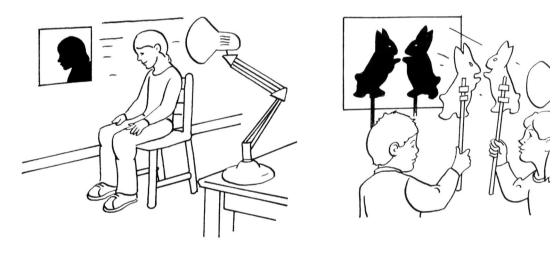

• **Figure 2.3:** Silhouettes

• **Figure 2.4:** Shadow puppets

Reflection and refraction

We are able to see most things because of light bouncing off them. Exactly how much light is reflected depends on the type of surface. A smooth white surface, for example, will obviously reflect more light than a dark, rough one. Because their surfaces are so smooth and shiny, mirrors are able to reflect light to give us a near perfect picture of an object and there are other shiny surfaces that also make good reflectors. Allow children to experiment with mirrors as a way of seeing objects in awkward situations.

- Where would you have to place a mirror to see someone who was standing behind you?
- How can mirrors be positioned to enable someone to see around the corner of a corridor?
- Why does the dentist use a small mirror?

Talk about how mirrors are used to carry out important safety tasks. Discuss the role of mirrors inside and outside a car and those used by motorists who have to manoeuvre out of difficult driveways. The photocopiable sheet *Up periscope* describes a periscope-making activity which uses mirrors to see over tall objects. Children may also be keen to find out how mirrors are used to produce patterns in a kaleidoscope.

Choose items from a collection of shiny objects and observe where they best pick up light.

- Can the highlights be made to move?
- Which objects can produce the image of a face?
- Is it always the same or is there any distortion?

A large polished serving spoon is particularly interesting. Ask children to look first into the bowl of the spoon, that is the concave surface. Get them to record the image.

- What happens then if the spoon is brought slowly up until it is very close to the eye?
- How do things change if the spoon is now held some distance away with the back, the convex surface, facing?

A little before Newton's experiments with light another scientist, Willebrord Snell, a Dutchman, discovered that when light travels from air into water strange things happen. Place a pencil or a straw into a glass of water and look down into the glass. The object appears to bend because the light bends as it enters water. This is called refraction (Figure 2.5). Examine the case of the disappearing button. Put a coloured button into the bottom of a cup and move back until it disappears from sight. Light from it is not reaching the eye. If water is then poured into the cup, the coin should reappear. It does so because the light from the coin has been refracted and now reaches the eye.

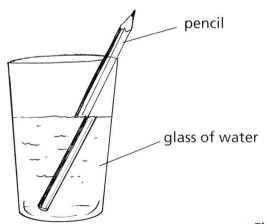

pencil

glass of water

• **Figure 2.5:** Refraction

SUPPORT

A number of difficult words are used in the activities. Provide a word bank to help with spellings and a glossary to help explain terms. Form small working groups carefully so that children are able to work together to support each other. Rely more on verbal feedback once children have carried out investigations and experiments. Get them to talk about what they have done and what they have found out. Provide a structured format for any written recording that has to be done.

EXTENSION

Expect children to devise their own criteria for what determines a fair test. Encourage them to develop and use their own simple tests and experiments when they are trying to find things out or investigate a theory they think may be true. During the work on shadows, see if small groups of children can make a sundial of some kind that will record the passing of time during the day. Set them other problem-solving tasks. For example, can they explain why some shops have a large curved mirror on one corner of the ceiling? Are they able to explain why cat's-eyes in the middle of the road are so effective?

KEY VOCABULARY

Source, LED (Light Emitting Diode), optic nerve, pupil, iris, retina, optical illusion, spectrum, prism, rainbow, droplet, transparent, translucent, opaque, shadow, profile, silhouette, sundial, reflection, reflector, refraction, periscope, kaleidoscope, highlight, distortion, concave, convex, image, disappear, reappear.

RESOURCES

Collection of different light sources – objects, photographs and pictures, collection of plastic mirrors, bubble-making set, glass jars, hose pipe, collection of papers and fabrics, collection of different glasses and plastics, oil, sandpaper, large sheet of white paper, desk lamp or projector, thin wooden rods, cardboard, sticks, shiny objects, large spoons, pencils, straws, buttons, cups, the photo-

---

NATIONAL CURRICULUM LINKS

Key Stage 2 Science

- Sc 1 Scientific enquiry: Ideas and evidence in science. 2 Investigative skills.
- Sc 4 Physical processes: 3 Light and sound – pupils should be taught (a) that light travels from a source; (b) that light cannot pass through some materials and how this leads to the formation of shadows; (c) that light is reflected from surfaces; (d) that we see things only when light from them enters our eyes.

Key Stage 2 Design and technology

- Developing, planning and communicating ideas.
- Working with tools, equipment, materials and components to make quality products.
- Evaluating processes and products.
- Breadth of study: during the key stage pupils should be taught the knowledge, skills and understanding through (a) investigating and evaluating a range of familiar products, thinking about how they work and how they are used; (c) design and make assignments using a range of materials.

ICT suggestions

Word processing for reports of experiments and investigations; use of cameras for photographic work; linking up light sensors to a computer for experiments.

Sometimes our eyes play tricks and we seem to see things
which are not there or which we know are not true.
Try these puzzles below.

Can you see spots?
Where do they appear?

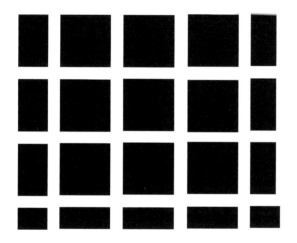

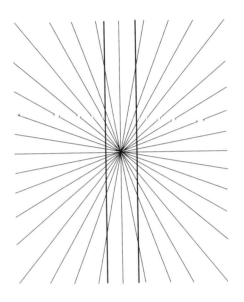

Are the two vertical lines straight?

Which line AB is longer?

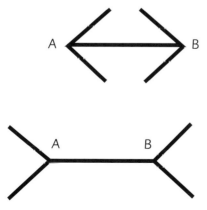

Can you see two faces in
profile or an ornate vase?

Periscopes help us to see over tall objects and around corners.

You will need: long thin cardboard cuboid box, glue, sticky tape, ruler, pencil, scissors, two small plastic mirrors.

Construct the periscope as shown in the diagram below

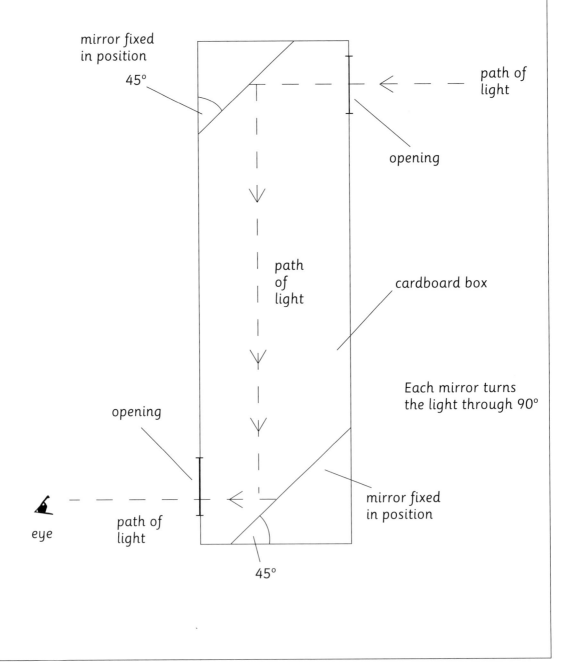

3
Michael Faraday
Turning on the power

Each year, around Christmas-time, a series of lectures is held in London to help children to understand scientific matters by explaining them in ordinary everyday language. The lectures – now televised to reach a much larger audience – are held at the Royal Institution and were first started in 1826 by one of its leading scientists, Michael Faraday.

Maybe the inspiration behind Faraday's decision to set up the lectures came from his own early life: he came from a poor family in the London suburb now known as the Elephant and Castle and was initially self-taught in physics and chemistry.

The son of a blacksmith, Faraday, who was born in 1791, had only a basic education before he started work as an errand-boy for a bookseller at the age of ten. Later he served a seven-year apprenticeship to become a bookbinder and his close daily contact with books gave him access to many subjects. Faraday became particularly fascinated by the books on chemistry and electricity that came to him for binding. In 1812 he was given some free tickets to attend a series of public lectures given by the eminent scientist Sir Humphrey Davy. This was to change the course of his life.

Faraday became so interested in the lectures that he took copious notes, bound them into a book and sent them to Davy, asking for a job as a laboratory assistant. The following year he became Davy's temporary assistant and, despite some conflict with Lady Davy, spent the next eighteen months touring a number of countries in Europe with Davy and his wife. Here Faraday developed his skills and knowledge through meeting many of the most important scientists of the time, including Volta, and discussing their work.

On his return to England, Faraday resumed his position as chemical assistant at the Royal Institution, helping not only Davy but also a number of other scientists who worked in its well-equipped laboratories. During 1816 and 1817 he assisted Davy in the development of the miner's lamp and then worked with James Stoddart on improving the quality of steel. But it was in 1821 that his career really began to take off following his promotion to Superintendent of the House. It was during this year, in one of the basement laboratories of the Institution, that Faraday started a series of experiments that led to his discovery of electromagnetic rotation, the principle behind the electric motor. Later he worked with the chemicals benzene and chlorine and undertook a project on making optical glass.

Remembering how stimulated he had been by Davy's lectures, Faraday began to organise and give public talks himself. Between 1826 and 1862 he gave over 120 Friday evening talks and there were nineteen series of Christmas lectures between 1827 and 1861. Both these series are still held today. Faraday was particularly fond of children and thought they made excellent scientists because they had open minds.

It was in August 1831 that Faraday made perhaps his most important discovery, electromagnetic induction. This lay behind the development of the electric transformer and generator and turned electricity from being just an interesting phenomenon for the scientist into a powerful and usable technology for all. He continued to work with electricity during the rest of the 1830s and in 1833 formulated his law of electrolysis, the breaking down of chemicals caused by the action of an electric current.

It was at this time that he was appointed scientific adviser to Trinity House, the organisation responsible for lighthouses around the coast of Britain. First he helped to improve the efficiency of the oil-burning lights and then experimented with, and tested out, several different systems of electric lighting. Faraday also taught chemistry to army officers and tried to make conditions safer for miners working underground. He always believed that the most important qualities a scientist should have were the ability to observe and perseverance.

His continuing work in science and for Trinity House began to affect his health. In 1858 he was given a pension and a house at Hampton Court near London by Queen Victoria and spent increasing amounts of time here in semi-retirement. He died in the house on 25 August 1867 and is buried in Highgate Cemetery.

CIRCUIT TRAINING

Discuss with the children the ways in which electricity is used within the home. List different rooms and itemise the electrical appliances that are used in each of them. Point out that electricity is an energy form that we cannot see but we know it is there because it makes things work. Sometimes electricity is able to make things work by making them hot, like a kettle element or a cooker hot plate. With other pieces of equipment it needs to operate a motor, as in a washing-machine, compact disc player or hairdryer. Talk about the purpose of plugs, sockets and switches and where they are positioned inside the home. Ask the children to find out where electricity comes from and how it is made.

- Do they know how the amount of electricity being used in their home is measured?
- Who provides it and how is it paid for?
- Talk about the importance of energy conservation at home and in school and what they can do to help.

This is also a good point, before experimentation takes place, to emphasise a number of important safety rules. Stress that the electricity supply into their homes is over 200 times stronger than the small batteries they use for work in school and is therefore extremely dangerous. Tell them never to use mains electricity for any of their investigations. Also reinforce, through discussion, other important safety rules about using electricity. Spend some time talking about the ideas on the photocopiable sheet *Be safe*. Here the children are asked to design and make a poster to alert people to some of the dangers involved.

Once this background work has been completed, provide small groups of children with the equipment needed to make simple circuits. Ask them to think about what they would need to light a small bulb. Make available bulbs, bulb holders, connecting wires, crocodile clips and batteries (4.5-volt torch batteries with clips on the top are easiest to connect up). Once they have successfully completed the task, ask them to find different ways of putting the bulb out. This will help them to understand that any break in the continuous metal pathway – in other words the circuit – will cause the bulb to go out. Unclipping a crocodile clip will do this, as will unscrewing the bulb. It will also help to prepare for later work on switches. Move on to experiment with different ways of connecting two bulbs to one battery. Make the test fair by ensuring that the bulbs are of equal rating – the same voltage and the same current. Before they start, ask the children if they can predict whether the two bulbs will be equally bright in any system they use. Most children will connect up the bulbs in what is known as a series circuit (Figure 3.1). Others may connect the bulbs as shown in Figure 3.2. This is called a parallel circuit.

- Can they think of other ways to connect them?
- Can they explain their results?
- What do they think will happen if one of the bulbs is unscrewed in each of the different circuits?

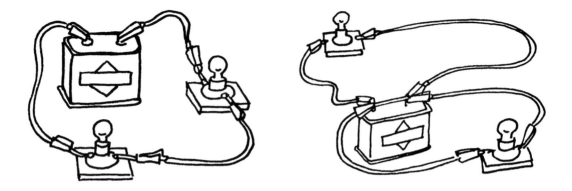

• **Figure 3.1:** Series circuit • **Figure 3.2:** Parallel circuit

Printed circuits that are made using tiny threads of wire are common in machines these days. One way of making a simple printed circuit is shown in Figure 3.3.

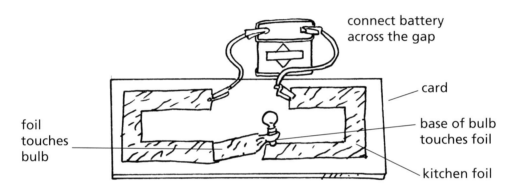

connect battery across the gap

card

foil touches bulb

base of bulb touches foil

kitchen foil

• **Figure 3.3:** Printed circuit

Encourage the children to record their efforts in diagram form so they have permanent details of their experiments once equipment has been taken apart and stored away. Some children will need to draw the actual items of equipment, showing clearly where connections are made while others may be capable of using symbols in place of pictures (Figure 3.4).

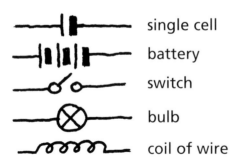

single cell

battery

switch

bulb

coil of wire

• **Figure 3.4:** Symbols used

Conductors and insulators

Move on to test a range of materials to see whether they are good conductors or insulators. Conductors permit the flow of electricity through them while insulators do not. After predictions have been made, the best way to carry out testing is to make up a circuit with a 'gap' in it. Then try various objects across the gap to see which conduct electricity and which are insulators. Experiment with different types of paper and card, plastic and wooden rulers, string, keys, paper-clips, erasers, rubber bands, plastic containers, pebbles, wool, plastic and paper straws, glass, aluminium foil, spoons, coins and china. Care needs to be taken with some objects that might have been painted. With a tin lid, for example, the metal underneath may be a good conductor, but the paint that covers it may act as an insulator. Take the opportunity to make children aware of the practical uses of their testing. It will help if you explain that, although they are covered to protect them, most electrical wires and cables are made of metal while plugs and switches contain large amounts of plastic.

Switched on

Switches permit control of the flow of electricity around a circuit. Children should experience a variety of switching mechanisms so that they will be able to make informed choices later about which ones suit any practical task they need to do. Initially, try simple versions like those using paper-clips and drawing pins (Figures 3.5 and 3.6). Then investigate pressure pads like the one shown in Figure 3.7. Other children may be able to branch out and try the clothes-peg model where the contacts may be broken by putting something between them (Figure 3.8). The 'tilt' switch (Figure 3.9) is made from a plastic 35mm film container that has a metal ball-bearing inside. If one is not available, try a ball of silver paper. Sticking up through the base of the container are small nails or panel pins to which two wires are connected. The wires go to the battery and to whatever is being made to work, a bulb, bell or buzzer. When the ball is rolled up to the lid end nothing works because no contact is being made. When it rolls down to touch the points of the two nails, the bulb, bell or buzzer comes on. The ball-bearing is now completing the circuit. Rolling the ball-bearing into the two positions, either to the lid or to the nails, makes the switch work on or off. The second tilt mechanism is similar to this except it involves rolling the

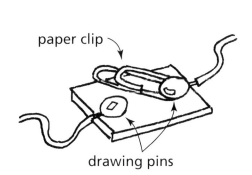

● **Figure 3.5:** Simple switches

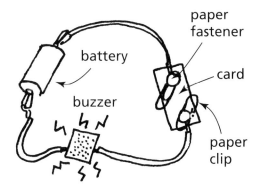

● **Figure 3.6:** Simple switches

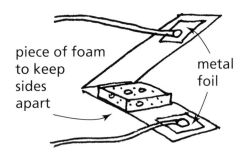

Figure 3.7: Pressure pad

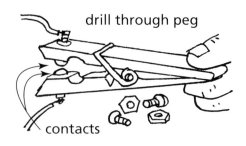

Figure 3.8: Peg switch

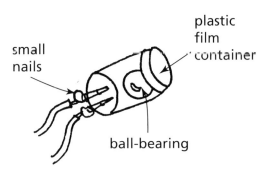

Figure 3.9: Tilt switch

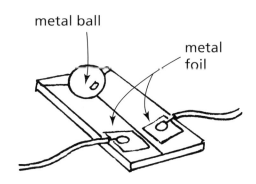

Figure 3.10: Second tilt switch

ball down a groove until it makes contact with the two metal foil strips (Figure 3.10). Children will need to make decisions about what kinds of switches and circuits to use when they try the practical activity described on the photocopiable sheet *Light it up!*

Magnetic attraction

It is claimed that Faraday became so concerned about the problem of producing electricity from magnetism that he always carried a magnet and a coil of wire around in his pocket to remind him.

Establish first of all that the children understand that magnets have two poles. One is south and the other is north. The north pole of a magnet is often marked with the capital letter N or by a dot. By bringing together matched pairs of magnets, children will be able to discover that like poles repel and unlike poles attract.

Collect as many items as possible and test them to see if they are attracted to a magnet. Test the magnet against fixtures in the room and record what happens (Figure 3.11). Magnets should, however, be kept away from delicate equipment that might be affected by them. Use the magnets to sort out mixtures like iron and brass screws and steel pins in sawdust. Test the strength of different types of magnet by seeing how many nails or paper clips they will hold (Figure 3.12). See if they work through other materials like paper, fabric, plastic and wood.

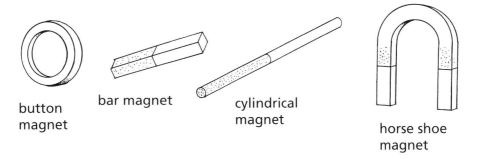

button
magnet

bar magnet

cylindrical
magnet

horse shoe
magnet

● **Figure 3.11:** Types of magents for testing

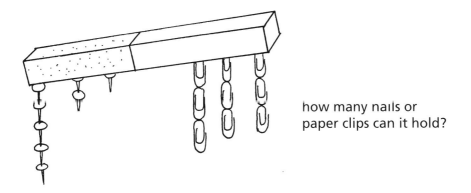

how many nails or
paper clips can it hold?

● **Figure 3.12:** Testing the strength of magnets

● Is it possible to move a nail inside a glass jar by using a magnet on the outside?

● Will a magnet pick up a small nail from the bottom of a bowl full of water without putting it into the water itself?

Electromagnets are used in places like scrapyards and recycling plants for moving cars or crushed metal. Children can make their own simple electromagnets using a battery, some copper wire and a large nail (see Figure 3.13). See how many pins or clips this kind of magnet can pick up. Does the number of turns of wire have any effect on the strength of the magnet produced?

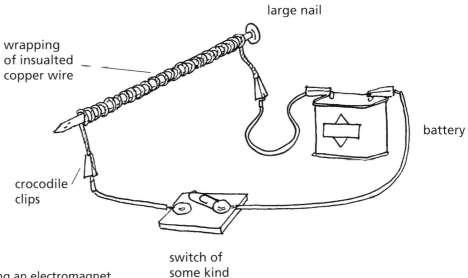

large nail

wrapping
of insualted
copper wire

battery

crocodile
clips

switch of
some kind

● **Figure 3.13:** Making an electromagnet

SUPPORT

Provide word banks when the children are listing electrical appliances found in the home. Room-plan sketches may help them to illustrate the distribution of different appliances. Reinforce work on safety rules by listing down key points. Assist with the setting up of different kinds of circuits especially series and parallel. Talk through what they have discovered rather than insisting on written conclusions. Help with the labelling of circuit drawings and provide key words. Provide recording sheets when children are carrying out testing, e.g. for conductors and insulators and sorting out magnetic and non-magnetic materials.

EXTENSION

Challenge the children to make practical devices using their knowledge of circuits and switches.

● Can they make models with flashing lights like lighthouses and traffic lights, for example?
● Can they design and make games where breaking the circuit causes something to happen, e.g. steady hand tester?
● Can they link their work up to a computer to provide more sophisticated forms of switching mechanisms?

Encourage all recording to be done using the recognised symbols. Ask the children to design and make games in which magnets are used to pick up objects, move them around or sort them out.

KEY VOCABULARY

Energy, electricity, plug, switch, socket, energy conservation, battery, circuit, bulb, bulb holder, bell, buzzer, wire, crocodile clip, volts, series circuit, parallel circuit, printed circuit, symbol, conductor, insulator, experiment, predict, pressure pad, tilt switch, magnets, magnetism, magnetic, non-magnetic, north pole, south pole, attract, repel, electromagnet.

RESOURCES

Examples of small electrical appliances for display, drawing paper, pencils, rulers, coloured pencils, felt pens, bulbs, bulb holders, wire, crocodile clips, 4.5v batteries, wire cutters, small screwdrivers, foil, plastic, wood, glass, china, wool, rubber, metal for testing conductors and insulators, paper-clips, drawing pins, nails, plastic containers, ball-bearings, silver paper, bells, buzzers, different types of magnet, range of items for testing magnetic and non-magnetic qualities, copper wire, large nail, other equipment may be needed for making electrical devices and/or magnetic games, etc., the photocopiable sheets *Be safe* and *Light it up!*

NATIONAL CURRICULUM LINKS

Key stage 2 Science

- Sc 1 Scientific enquiry: 1 Ideas and evidence in science. 2 Investigative skills.
- Sc 3 Materials and their properties: 1 Grouping and classifying materials – pupils should be taught (b) that some materials are better thermal insulators than others; (c) that some materials are better electrical conductors than others.
- Sc 4 Physical processes: 1 Electricity – pupils should be taught (a) to construct circuits incorporating a battery or power supply and a range of switches to make electrical devices work; (b) how changing the number or type of components in a series circuit can make bulbs brighter or dimmer; (c) how to represent series circuits in drawings and conventional symbols and how to construct series circuits on the basis of drawings and diagrams using conventional symbols. 2 Forces and motion – pupils should be taught (a) about forces of attraction and repulsion between magnets and about the forces of attraction between magnets and magnetic materials.

Key Stage 2 Design and technology

- Developing, planning and communicating ideas.
- Working with tools, equipment, materials and components to make quality products.
- Evaluating processes and products.
- Knowledge and understanding of materials and components: pupils should be taught (d) how electrical circuits, including those with simple switches, can be used to achieve results that work.
- Breadth of study: during the key stage, pupils should be taught the knowledge, skills and understanding through (a) investigating and evaluating a range of familiar products, thinking about how they work, how they are used and the views of people who use them; (c) designing and making assignments using a range of materials, including electrical and mechanical components.

ICT suggestions

Word processing for investigation reports; use of appropriate software to control working models; use of computer for switching mechanisms for bulbs, buzzers and motors.

• Every year many accidents happen in the home because electricity is not used safely.

• Design and draw a poster in the box encouraging people to use electricity safely. Use large bold lettering and some interesting pictures or diagrams. Some possible ideas are given at the bottom of the sheet.

• overloading sockets   • frayed wires   • cracked plugs   • water and electricity

You are going to build a model that will light up in some way.
Some ideas are given below.

• Think about what type of electrical circuit you will use and decide
  on the best type of switch.
• Use a range of equipment including bulbs, bulb holders, batteries, wires,
  crocodile clips.

Idea 1: Home sweet home

light up a model room

Idea 2: Glowing monster

make his
eyes
shine
brightly

Idea 3: Safety at sea

make the
light flash
its warning
message

Idea 4: Traffic lights

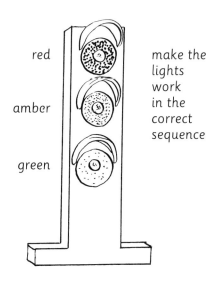

red

amber

green

make the
lights
work
in the
correct
sequence

Samuel Morse

Sounding out the message

It is a widely-held belief that those who listen in or eavesdrop on other people's conversations rarely hear anything to their advantage, and often the reverse. The American scientist and inventor Samuel Finley Breeze Morse would certainly not agree. Morse did his listening while he was crossing the Atlantic Ocean by steamer after a visit to Europe in 1832 and it was as a result of the information he overheard about the properties of electromagnets that he decided on a significant history-making career change.

Born in Charlestown in the USA in 1791, Morse was the son of a minister who was also the author of some of the first books on geography. He graduated from Yale University in 1810 and spent the first part of his working life earning his living as an artist in both America and Europe. Morse lived in England between 1811 and 1815 and exhibited some of his work at the Royal Academy. He specialised in painting portraits, especially miniatures.

Following the overheard conversation, Morse decided to abandon his painting and many of his other interests and, in partnership with some of his friends, give the development of the electric telegraph his full attention. He had little money to start with and was forced to make all his own models and spare parts.

His research was based on work done earlier by a Danish scientist named Hans Christian Oersted, who had noticed the effects an electric current had on a compass needle. Morse discovered that an electric current, supplied from a battery working an electromagnet, was able to cause a pencil to mark a moving strip of paper. The supply was turned on and off by a simple key. Pressing down the key caused the current to flow while releasing it stopped the current. He also noticed that long taps on the key caused long electrical pulses and short taps produced short pulses. It was from this discovery that the system known as Morse Code developed. Long pulses could be represented by dashes, short ones by dots. Each letter of the alphabet, the digits from 0 to 9 and important punctuation marks were represented by a unique combination of dashes and dots. (See the photocopiable sheet *Cracking the code*.)

At first, Morse had trouble getting people to accept his ideas, and for a long time the United States government refused to back the scheme with money. Eventually, financial help was granted and the first message using Morse's electric telegraph system was sent on 24 May 1844. The phrase 'What God hath wrought' was transmitted from the Supreme Court Room in the Capitol in Washington to the railway depot at Baltimore, a distance of sixty kilometres (thirty-seven miles). It seems to us now a primitive method of sending messages but it became, in effect, the information superhighway of the mid-nineteenth century and in many ways started the whole communications revolution. Within a matter of years, Morse's machine, his landline system and the code he invented to speed up the sending of messages, were influencing the way of life of many people. The code opened up business, financial and political communications in the USA and was soon used by journalists, especially through agencies like the Associated Press and Reuters to report the news. It was first used by the military during the Crimean War and the American Civil War and many rescues, especially at sea, were planned and carried out through the use of the code. Although radio signals took over at the beginning of the twentieth century, the code itself only stopped being used for distress calls by large ships in February 1999, when a global satellite communications system took its place.

Others were quick to try and make a profit from Morse's inventions and he argued that instead of making him wealthy his discoveries often cost him money because of the legal cases he had to fight to protect his findings. Later he found the right investors who would provide money for the spread of his communications system. One company he became involved with was the American Telegraph Company, which by 1858 was making plans to lay the first transatlantic cable under the ocean from Newfoundland to the coast of Ireland. America was soon to be linked to Europe.

Towards the end of his life, Morse, who was married twice and had eight children, travelled throughout Europe with his family and was honoured and rewarded wherever he went. In 1871 a special statue of him was unveiled in Central Park, New York, and he died a year later at the age of eighty.

SURROUNDED BY SOUND

Sound is a phenomenon that children easily appreciate. They can hear it, often feel it and even, on occasions, see the effects of it. They need to understand that it is a form of energy and that for sound to be produced vibrations must be set up from some kind of source. These vibrations travel through the air in waves and some of them enter the ear where they are heard. Vibrations that have a lot of energy sound loud while those with little energy sound quiet. In general terms, the longer the wave the deeper the sound will be, while larger waves produce greater volume (see Figure 4.1).

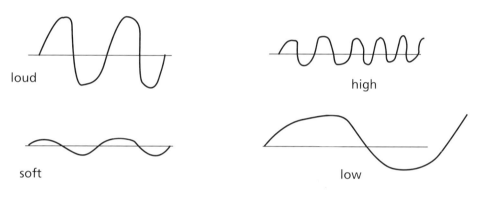

● **Figure 4.1:** Sound waves

Start the work on sound by asking children to collect the sounds that they can hear around them both indoors and outdoors, around the school, in the street and at home. Can they classify them into loud and quiet or pleasant and unpleasant? Ask them to try and describe the sounds in words. They should be able to distinguish, for example, between a rustle and a squeak and while both a crash and a clang may both be loud sounds, they should have certain distinctive features. List all those well-known phrases that are connected to sound in some way, e.g. 'You could hear a pin drop' and 'It's all very hush, hush'. Discuss how sounds can be used to good effect in alliterative poems (Figure 4.2) and how they feature strongly in stories told in cartoon fashion (Figure 4.3).

Crunching, clashing, crashing
   crocodiles

Buzzing, bashing, battling
   bumble bee

● **Figure 4.2:** Alliterative sound poems

● **Figure 4.3:** Cartoon sound

Check how good their hearing skills are by asking a group of children with a tape recorder to gather different sounds from around the school.

- How many of the sounds can the other children recognise?
- Are some of the sounds easier to pick out than others?
- Is general background noise a problem?

Extend this activity by enriching stories and plays with suitable sound effects, always remembering that some sound effects can be produced in quite different ways, e.g. coconut shells for horses' hooves. Ask the children to devise fair tests to see how good their hearing really is.

- Can a child wearing a blindfold correctly point in the direction a sound is coming from?
- Is it easier to hear sound from in front or from behind?
- Are different results produced because of the type of sound that has been used?

Do not miss the chance to talk about how animals make sounds and the reasons why they do it. Contrast the cricket rubbing its back legs together with the gorilla beating its chest, for example. Look at the shape and position of animals' ears and how many are specially adapted to improve hearing.

The highs and lows of sound

Investigate different ways of making sounds and the way in which these can be modified or changed. Use simple items found around the classroom. Focus first on making sound vibrations by hitting, tapping, plucking or blowing objects. Try tapping out a rhythm on a tabletop with a pencil. Pluck a rubber band stretched over an open box or vibrate a ruler sticking out over the edge of a table. Alternatively, investigate blowing across the top of a bottle, sprinkling some seeds on the top of a drum or blowing between two pieces of paper held between the hands.

Then experiment with the pitch and volume of sounds. The pitch of a note – that is how high or low it is – depends on the speed of the vibrations. Loudness is determined by the size of the vibration. The bigger the vibration the louder the sound. Ask a child to run a fingernail slowly along the teeth of a comb and listen to the scraping noise it produces. Now repeat the process quickly and note changes in sound. Run a pencil across a piece of corrugated card (Figure 4.4). Children should be able to detect how the note goes up as the speed increases. In small groups, children can vibrate rulers sticking out over the edge of a table. What results do they get if they vary the length of the part of the ruler that is over the edge, the force of the twang or the way they hold the other end of the ruler? Do strips of other materials respond in the same way? (Figure 4.5.) Look into the way certain factors can be used to alter pitch. Set up the experiment shown in Figure 4.6. Vary the tightness or tension of the band using weights and change the length of the band by moving the position of the pencils. Encourage children to predict what might happen once the arrangement has been changed but before they have tested it out. What effect does changing the thickness of the band have? Perform identical tests using different types of string, fishing-line and thin wire. Try the water in the bottle activity shown in Figure 4.7. Get children to blow gently across the top of an empty bottle to see what sound is produced.

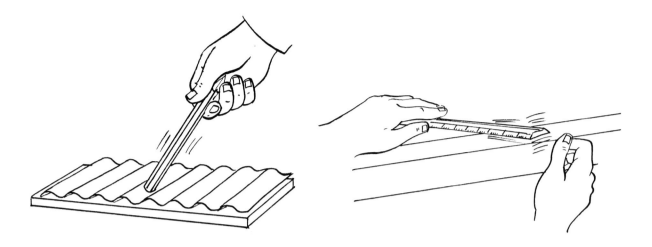

● **Figure 4.4:** Pencil on corrugated paper

● **Figure 4.5:** Ruler and table

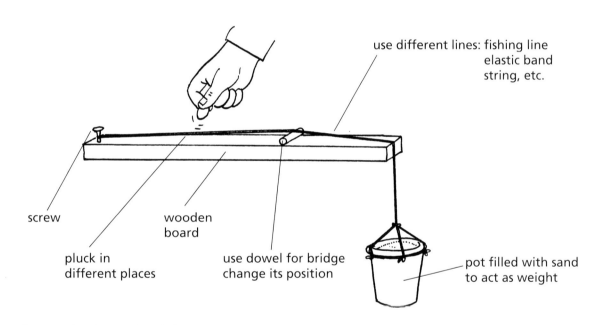

use different lines: fishing line
elastic band
string, etc.

screw

wooden board

pluck in different places

use dowel for bridge change its position

pot filled with sand to act as weight

● **Figure 4.6:** Change the pitch

Does the amount of water change the sound? How?

● **Figure 4.7:** Water in the bottles

- What happens to the sound if water is poured into the bottle?
- If the bottle is tapped is the pitch of the sound the same?
- Vary the conditions even more. Does standing the bottle on different surfaces change things?
- Does the kind of liquid inside the bottle make any difference?

Loudness usually depends on the size of the vibrations. Hit a drum gently, then hit it hard. The harder it is hit, the bigger the vibrations of the drum skin and the louder it will sound. See if other instruments like a guitar and a recorder react in the same way. It is also worth pointing out, though, that the distance between the sound and the listener will also have some effect on the volume. This is because sound spreads out in all directions once it leaves its source. The photocopiable sheet *Let's make music* gives children the chance to make their own sound instruments.

Travelling sound

It may surprise some children that solids are very good transmitters of sound. They are better than liquids, which in turn perform better than gases. Check out how sound travels through different materials.

- Is it possible to hear approaching feet better with an ear to the ground?
- Can sounds be passed along heating pipes from one room to another?
- Is it possible to make sounds travel along a brick wall?

Encourage children to make a simple stethoscope (Figure 4.8) that they can use to listen to sounds travelling through different materials. Also consider the way in which materials will either reflect or absorb sound. Reflection tends to be increased by hard, smooth surfaces and reduced by those that are softer and more irregular. Talk about what happens to sound inside a confined space like a tunnel, how echo sounders work on ships and how some creatures like bats rely on reflected sound to help them move around safely. Others, like whales, communicate with each other over long distances underwater.

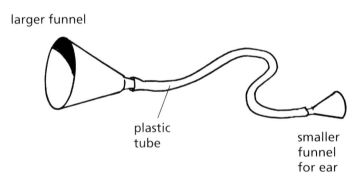

larger funnel

plastic
tube

smaller
funnel
for ear

● **Figure 4.8:** Simple stethoscope

Challenge children to see whether they can improve the way in which sound travels over long distances outside.

- If they talk through a long thin tube does it make it easier for others to hear? Who can design and make the most effective megaphone?
- What shape does it need to be?
- What is the best material to make it from?
- Do weather conditions make any difference to its performance? (See Figure 4.9.)

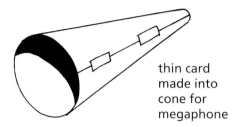

thin card
made into
cone for
megaphone

● **Figure 4.9:** Megaphone

Activities using string telephones can lead to lots of worthwhile investigations (Figure 4.10). Encourage children to think up their own questions to be investigated. Try a variety of strings or other long thin materials.

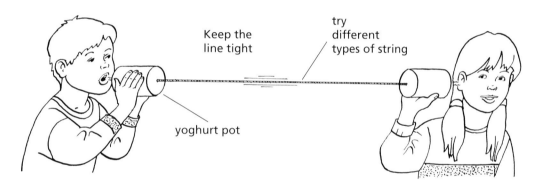

Keep the
line tight

try
different
types of string

yoghurt pot

● **Figure 4.10:** String telephone

- Does the string need to be tight?
- What happens if the string is knotted?
- Does the shape and material of the containers matter?
- Over what kind of distances does the 'telephone' work?
- Will it work around corners?

SUPPORT

Many of the activities will require the children to devise their own fair tests. Support and assist as much as possible by providing them with definite questions to use. For example, for activities like sounds travelling through different materials, ask questions like these: What will sound go through? Can you find out if sound will travel through metal? Also provide headed tables when children are being asked to record results. Discuss their findings with them verbally and cut down on the amount of written recording needed. Locate materials in well-labelled storage containers so that children can find and use them easily.

EXTENSION

When children are working on simple experiments, encourage them to develop their own lines of enquiry by asking more open-ended questions, and also to extend their work through research, some of which can be carried out in their own time. Some may be interested in the link between sound and musical instruments. Others could investigate how sound has been used throughout history to communicate with others and convey messages. Other possible units of work could include animal sounds, or the way in which sound vibrations are transmitted by electrical means.

KEY VOCABULARY

Sound, energy, vibration, source, loud, quiet, volume, sound words (e.g. rustle, squeak, clang, crash), ear muffs, soundproofing, sound phrases (e.g. sounds good to me), background noise, sound effects, distance, rhythm, pitch, high, low, speed, tightness, tension, transmit, transmitters, solid, liquid, gas, travel, materials, stethoscope, reflect, absorb, echo, megaphone, telephone.

RESOURCES

Tape recorder, blindfold, items to create sound effects, reference books to research animal sounds, sound communications, modern communications, pencils, rulers, rubber bands, glass bottles, plastic containers, seeds, paper, card, musical instruments (pitched and unpitched), comb, range of different materials for sound tests, string, fishing-line, thin wire, rubber tubing, cardboard tubes, supply of water for bottles, photocopiable sheets *Cracking the code* and *Let's make music*.

NATIONAL CURRICULUM LINKS

Key Stage 2 Science

- Sc 1 Scientific enquiry: 1 Ideas and evidence in science. 2 Investigative skills.
- Sc 4 Physical processes: 3 Light and sound – pupils should be taught (e) that sounds are made when objects vibrate but that vibrations are not always directly visible; (f) how to change pitch and loudness of sounds produced by some vibrating objects; (g) that vibrations from sound sources require a medium through which to travel to the ear.

Key Stage 2 Design and technology

- Developing, planning and communicating ideas.
- Working with tools, equipment, materials and components to make quality products.
- Evaluating processes and products.
- Breadth of study: during the key stage pupils should be taught the knowledge, skills and understanding through (c) designing and making assignments using a range of materials.

ICT suggestions

Use of word processor for reports of investigations; use of tape recorders for collecting sounds; use of electronic keyboard for making up sounds and compositions; use of computer to compose musical sounds.

- This is the Morse Code invented by Samuel Morse and his friends for sending quick messages along the electric telegraph.
- Each letter of the alphabet has a series of dots and dashes.

A • —	I • •	Q — — • —	Y — • — —
B — • • •	J • — — —	R • — •	Z — — • •
C — • — •	K — • —	S • • •	
D — • •	L • — • •	T —	
E •	M — —	U • • —	
F • • — •	N — •	V • • • —	
G — — •	O — — —	W • — —	
H • • • •	P • — — •	X — • • —	

- What does this message say?

• • • , • — , — — , • • — , • , • — • • / — — , — — — , • — • , • • • , • /

• — — , • — , • • • / • — , — — • , • — • , • • , — • — • , • — , — •

- Write your name in Morse Code.

- Turn this message into Morse Code.
  We are sinking. Please send help.

- Can you make up your own code system?

- Create interesting and tuneful sounds by making your own musical instruments.
- Collect the materials you will need.
- Some suggestions are given below.

Instruments you can blow

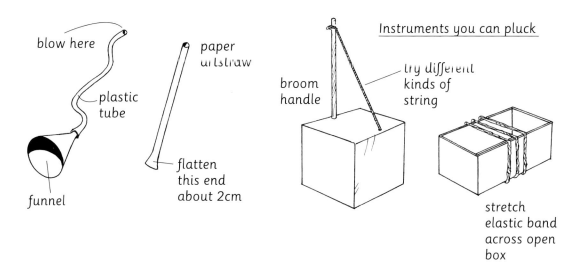

blow here

plastic tube

funnel

paper or straw

flatten this end about 2cm

Instruments you can pluck

broom handle

try different kinds of string

stretch elastic band across open box

Instruments you can shake

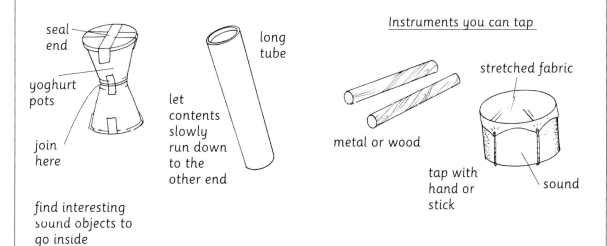

seal end

yoghurt pots

join here

find interesting sound objects to go inside

long tube

let contents slowly run down to the other end

Instruments you can tap

metal or wood

stretched fabric

tap with hand or stick

sound

5

Karl Benz

Building the engines

No one could have blamed Karl Benz if he had grown up with a lifelong hatred of machines and engines, for soon after he was born in 1844 his father was the first engine driver ever to be killed in a railway accident.

But far from hating mechanical things, Benz enjoyed working with them. He started to train as a fitter at the Karlsruhe steam engine works in Germany as soon as he was old enough to leave school and then spent the rest of his working life designing and building motor cars. He was dedicated to the idea that the engines he worked on would supersede the horse and radically change world transportation. He fervently believed it was possible to take the chemical energy produced from fuel and turn it into the kinetic energy needed to make an object move.

It is difficult to establish who exactly was the first person to perfect a robust enough petrol-driven internal combustion engine to power the first cars. Benz was certainly among them but there were a number of rivals at the time, including fellow Germans Gottlieb Daimler, Nikolaus Otto and Wilhelm Maybach as well as Etienne Lenoir in France. Benz was without doubt the first to develop the manufacturing process all the way through to the finished car and this led to the production of the Benz Motorwagen in 1886.

The original Benz car, which can still be viewed today in a Munich museum, had only three wheels. Built on a steel frame in the shape of a horseshoe, it was based on a two-seater horse cart with a small engine at the rear. The driver and single passenger were completely open to the weather. It was steered by means of a tiller and stopped by a hard pull on the single handbrake lever. The wheels – two large ones at the back and a smaller one at the front – were spoked like bicycle wheels and the solid rubber tyres made it quite an uncomfortable ride. The engine, complete with a huge flywheel, was at the back of the car. The parts of the bodywork that were not constructed of metal were made out of wood and the seats were made of leather. After special permission was granted to allow the car on the road, it was first driven in public in July 1886 at Mannheim in Germany, when a speed of fifteen kilometres per hour was reached.

The famous engineer's wife, Berthe, was also fanatical about cars. Soon after the revolutionary vehicle had gone into production, she made the first ever long distance drive over a route of 100 kilometres. She took their two teenage sons, Richard and Eugene, with her. They were forced to stop several times for repairs on the way. As there were no garages at the time to help them one of the stops involved a visit to a blacksmith.

From its early beginnings the Benz factory quickly grew in size. By 1888, despite having trouble finding backers to put up the money, fifty men were employed to work there. Production of a four-wheeled vehicle called the Victoria was started in 1893 and an interest in racing cars developed after one of Benz's machines took part in the first recorded car race the following year. For a time a 200 horsepower car built by the Benz Company held the world land speed record.

Later, in 1926, with financial problems in Germany at their height and the need to fight strong opposition from car makers in the United States, the firm, after several earlier unsuccessful attempts, was merged with the Daimler Company to form Daimler-Benz and Co. The name was soon changed, however, to the now more familiar Mercedes Benz when one of the company bosses decided to use his daughter's name because he thought the German sounding name might affect sales of the car in neighbouring France. The company went on to produce trucks and lorries and also became the first to introduce diesel passenger vehicles.

By this time Benz had left to work in partnership with his two sons. He remained active in the car business until his death in 1929 at the age of eighty-five.

ON THE MOVE

Forces are at work all around us and although we cannot see them we can see the effects they have. It is a force that makes stationary objects move. It makes moving objects speed up or slow down. Forces cause changes in direction and can bend, twist or alter the shapes of things. Forces can be very small, like the ant carrying the leaf back to its nest, or huge, like the four massive engines needed to lift a jet airliner off the ground.

Spend some time discussing with the children what they understand by the word 'force'. Examine the meaning of a number of key words that are likely to occur during practical work on forces. Make them aware that some forces have special names. Gravity, for example, is the force that pulls everything towards the centre of the planet. Some children will know, however, that in space there is zero gravity, which causes the phenomenon referred to as weightlessness. Friction, on the other hand, is the force that acts to prevent movement when two surfaces are rubbed together. Talk about natural forces like air, wind and water. Explain that machines, or more specifically the mechanisms within them, usually permit jobs to be done with less force.

Levers can alter the amount of force that is being applied and pulleys are used to change the direction and amount of a force.

Also ensure that children are confident about the way in which forces can be measured with a force meter or spring balance. Check that they are able to read the calibration shown on measuring equipment correctly. They will need to know that force is measured in Newtons – the name being taken from the famous scientist who is featured in another chapter of this book. One Newton is equal to the weight of about 100 grams, the equivalent of an average-sized apple.

Develop the work on forces with a detailed look at the bicycle. Ask one of the children to obtain permission to bring their bicycle into school. There are many advantages to using this as a teaching aid. Bicycles are easily accessible and are machines that all children are familiar with. Most, if not all, working parts are clearly visible. Discuss the forces involved in starting, stopping, going slowly, turning corners and travelling down a bumpy road. Ask the children to record what they do and the forces they feel when they are riding, turning, stopping or starting.

- What do they notice?
- Where do they push?
- When do they need to pull?

Get them to analyse what happens as a result of their force.

- Are different forces used at different times?
- What effect does the force have?
- Is the push or pull passed on to other parts of the bicycle?
- When and where can they feel opposing pushes and pulls?
- How could they apply this to the words 'action' and 'reaction'?

Take the opportunity to look at the wheels in some detail.

- What are they made of?
- How are they strengthened?
- How are they attached to the frame?
- How do they move?
- Which is the 'driven' wheel and which is the 'free' one?

Compare the wheels found on a skateboard, roller blades and other children's toys with wheels.

- How many wheels do they have?
- Where are they positioned?
- Are axles used to attach the wheels?
- How do they help the machine to run smoothly?

If children are to make models that have wheels they will need time to explore ways in which the wheels can be fitted successfully to the chassis or body. Some ideas and suggestions are given in Figure 5.1. Look at the special wheels on the bicycle known as cogwheels. Why are they different sizes and why do they have teeth? Study other mechanisms that have cogwheels where teeth have been placed around the edge to interlink with those on similar wheels. Hand drills, egg whisks and old clock wheels are good examples. Why is the use of teeth so important? Models incorporating cogwheels can be made from construction kits. One way of making your own versions of them in the classroom is shown in Figure 5.2.

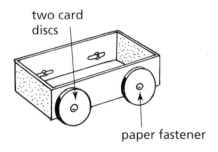

two card discs

paper fastener

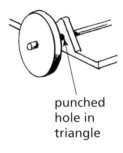

punched hole in triangle

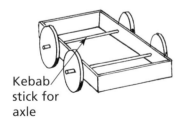

Kebab stick for axle

sticky tape used to secure axle

• **Figure 5.1:** Ideas for fitting wheels to the body of a vehicle

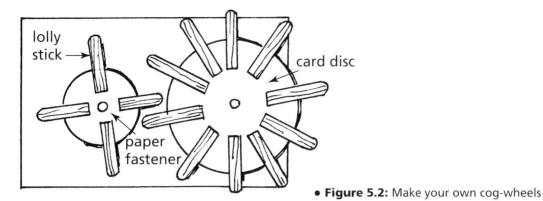

● **Figure 5.2:** Make your own cog-wheels

Pulleys are grooved wheels that are used to pull or hoist weights of some kind. Collect pictures and photographs to illustrate them and discuss how they are used on a range of items including cranes, sailing craft and roller blinds. If commercially produced pulleys are available, they can be used for a variety of lifting and lowering tasks. Alternatively, simple pulleys can be made from materials that are easy to gather (Figure 5.3). Grooves or ridges on the wheels are important to prevent string from slipping and the thickness and texture of a string itself also affects performance.

Slide a cotton reel on to a metal coathanger

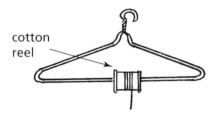

A sturdier but more complicated alternative

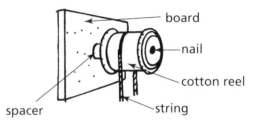

● **Figure 5.3:** Making simple pulleys

Levers are often used to make a force acting in one direction produce a movement in another direction. Return to the bicycle and investigate how levers are used to operate the braking system and in many cases to change gear. Examine door handles and catches, tin and bottle openers, screwdrivers and hammers with parts designed to remove nails. Then demonstrate how pairs of levers work together in pliers, scissors, tongs, clothes pegs and nutcrackers. One way to get children to experiment with levers is to ask them to make models that involve balance at a fulcrum or those that have moving parts. Some simple ideas are shown in Figure 5.4 and a more detailed assignment is provided on the photocopiable sheet *Getting mobile*.

Slowing things down

Children who cannot easily slide a large box over the floor surface or have had to stop tobogganing because the snow has almost disappeared will appreciate the negative side of friction. But it can have its uses too. We need high friction, for

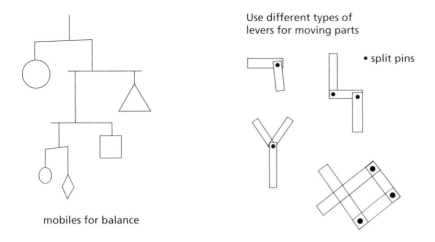

Use different types of
levers for moving parts

• split pins

mobiles for balance

• **Figure 5.4:** Using levers/balance and moving parts

example, to run with trainers on or to stop a bicycle using our brakes, and low friction to skate or use a playground slider.

Ask the children to investigate which surfaces heavy objects will slide along more easily (Figure 5.5). Use a brick or something similar. Attach string to the brick and pull it along the table. Record the reading on the force meter in Newtons. In general terms, the higher the reading the greater the force being used. Change the surface of the brick by wrapping materials like plastic or sandpaper around it. What happens now? Change the surface of the table by placing paper or carpet under the brick. Does this change the results? Make a sloping surface by using a wooden board (Figure 5.6). Is it easier pulling up or down the slope? Discuss the role of lubrication. Throughout this activity it is important that children predict what they think will happen and then carry out a fair test. Measurements will need to be taken and recorded carefully and then related to their predictions before conclusions are drawn. An experiment that extends this activity and also looks at ways of trying to overcome friction is given on the photocopiable sheet *Make it slide.*

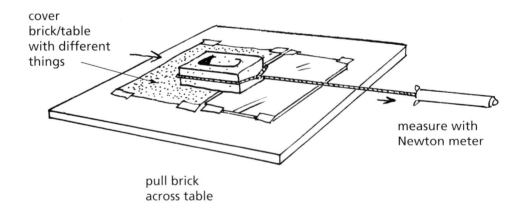

cover
brick/table
with different
things

measure with
Newton meter

pull brick
across table

• **Figure 5.5:** Moving the brick

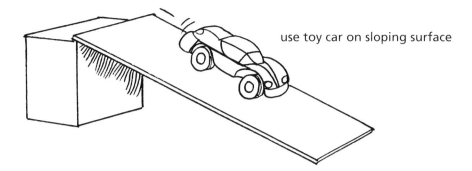

use toy car on sloping surface

• **Figure 5.6:** Sloping surface

Natural forces like air, wind and water can also slow movement down. Explore and investigate parachutes, for example. Take identical sheets of paper and drop them. Try a piece that is flat, one that is crumpled and others that have been folded into a range of different shapes.

● What differences are there in the way that they fall?
● Are any patterns evident that will help the children to predict what might happen?
● What is the best way to time the fall?
● Does the type of paper used affect the outcome?

Then pose the question 'what makes the best parachute?' (Figure 5.7). Try different papers and fabrics in different sizes and with different weights on the end of the string.

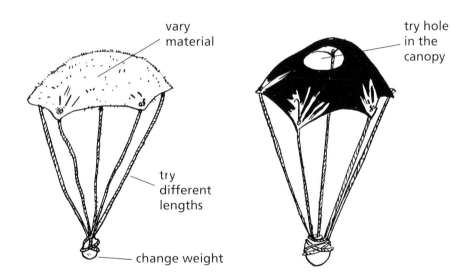

vary material

try hole in the canopy

try different lengths

change weight

• **Figure 5.7:** Parachutes

● Is the length of the string important?
● Does a hole in the canopy make any difference?
● Does the size of the surface area of the parachute affect how fast it falls?

Tabulating the results carefully should help to produce the combination of factors that proves to be most successful.

Then take groups of children outside and ask them to run across the playground with a large sheet of cardboard held in front of them. First hold the board up so that it faces the wind. Try the same thing with the board held end on (Figure 5.8). Can the children feel the difference? Talk about walking and riding a bicycle on a windy day as a way of introducing the term 'air resistance'.

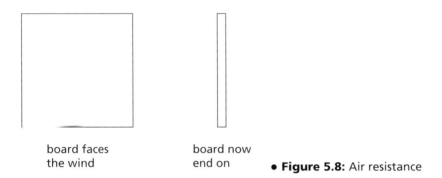

board faces
the wind

board now
end on

● **Figure 5.8:** Air resistance

Any child who has waded through water in the shallow end of the swimming pool or been knocked off their feet while jumping the waves at the seaside will realise the power of water resistance. Drop the same piece of Plasticine made into different shapes down into a cylinder filled with water and time how long it takes to fall. Ensure the test is kept fair. Link discussion here with the tests carried out on hull shapes in chapter 1 (Brunel). Talk about how the force of wind and water can often be made to work for us but that on other occasions objects have to be streamlined in order to minimise the effects of the force they exert.

SUPPORT

Revise and reinforce the key words and vocabulary needed to carry out these activities. Work with children to make sure they can use force meters and spring balances successfully and they are able to read off measurements accurately. Matching up children into mixed ability groups may help this process. Give children specific questions to find the answers to and provide structured tables to be used when they are collecting results and gathering information. Have a range of materials and equipment available for the children to use when they are carrying out experiments. Encourage the use of drawings and diagrams to show results rather than putting the accent entirely on written recording.

EXTENSION

When talking about different kinds of forces, encourage children to work out questions for themselves. Help them extend tasks given to them by devising their own investigations. Expect more refined prediction skills and well-argued conclusions. Ask children to carry out research by using books, pictures and the computer to find ways in which they could apply their findings to practical, ordinary, everyday life situations. Can they, for example, use either air or water resistance to make something work, e.g. a waterwheel, or design a streamlined method of transport?

KEY VOCABULARY

Force, stationary, direction, gravity, zero gravity, weightlessness, friction, force meter, spring balance, Newton, surface area, machine, mechanism, push, pull, action, reaction, frame, chassis, body, axle, hub, cogwheel, pulley, lever, energy, effort, fulcrum, balance, lubrication, air resistance, water resistance, streamlining, aerodynamic.

RESOURCES

Force meters, spring balances, bicycle, skateboards, roller blades, toys with wheels, equipment for making models with wheels, drills, egg whisks, old clock mechanisms, pulley wheels, string, cotton reels, bottle openers, handles and catches, pliers, scissors, tongs, clothes pegs, house bricks, different materials and fabrics, wooden board, paper, small weights, large sheet of cardboard, Plasticine, cylinders, the photocopiable sheets *Getting mobile* and *Making it slide*.

NATIONAL CURRICULUM LINKS

Key Stage 2 Science

- Sc 1 Scientific enquiry: 1 Ideas and evidence in science. 2 Investigative skills.
- Sc 4 Physical processes: 2 Forces and motion – pupils should be taught (b) that objects are pulled downwards because of the gravitational attraction between them and the Earth; (c) about friction, including air resistance as a force that slows moving objects and may prevent objects from starting to move; (d) that when objects are pushed and pulled an opposing pull or push can be felt; (e) how to measure forces and identify the direction in which they act.

Key Stage 2 Design and technology

- Developing, planning and communicating ideas.
- Working with tools, equipment, materials and components to make quality products.
- Evaluating processes and products.
- Knowledge and understanding of materials and components: pupils should be taught (c) how mechanisms can be used to make things move in different ways.
- Breadth of study: during the key stage pupils should be taught the knowledge, skills and understanding through (a) investigating and evaluating a range of familiar products, thinking about how they work and how they are used; (c) designing and making assignments using a range of materials.

ICT suggestions

Word processing for reports of investigations; use of simple databases to record information; use of appropriate software to control working models.

Challenge

Design and make a car, cart or buggy which can be used to carry objects.

• Try as many different types of wheel systems as you can.
• The wheels should be able to move as freely as possible.
• Test the model to see how it moves on different surfaces.

Design and plan your model in a fully labelled sketch here:

You will need a wooden block, 1kg weight, hook, elastic band.

Set up the experiment as shown in the picture.
You will measure the stretch in the elastic band to give the pull needed to start the block moving.
Different surfaces and surface conditions will be used.

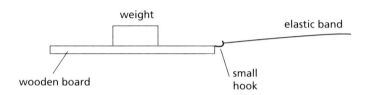

weight

elastic band

wooden board

small hook

Record your results like this:

Surface tested	Length of pull needed
Plastic desk top – dry	
Plastic desk top + water	
Plastic desk top + oil	
Plastic desk top + washing-up liquid	
Playground – dry	
Playground + water	
Playground + oil	
Playground + washing-up liquid	

Add others of your own here ⟶

Discuss what you have found out about friction

6
Marie Curie
Discovering new elements

Marie Curie, believed by many to be the greatest woman scientist who has ever lived, once said, 'Nothing in life is to be feared. It is only to be understood.' It was a motto she certainly put into practice.

From her early days in Poland when she had to struggle to be accepted even as a student, Marie Curie rose to attain a wealth of notable firsts. She became the first woman in Europe to receive a doctorate of science, the first woman to teach at the world-famous Sorbonne University in Paris and the first woman to win a Nobel Prize for physics. She gave several new words to the dictionary and the list could go on.

She was born in the Polish capital Warsaw in 1867. Well known for her prodigious memory, Marie did well at school. Polish universities were not allowed to take women at that time and her parents, despite both being teachers, did not have sufficient money to send her to university abroad. To raise the necessary funds, Marie worked first as a teacher and then as a governess, also finding time to read at secret meetings to women workers who had joined the so-called 'free university'.

In 1891 she moved to Paris to study science at the Sorbonne. It was a time of great hardship. She devoted all her energy to studying, lived in a tiny attic room at the top of a large house and seems to have survived on a diet of bread, butter and tea. She obtained a degree in mathematical sciences in 1894 and the following year married another scientist she had met at the Sorbonne called Pierre Curie. It was a partnership that was soon to make discoveries of world importance.

The Curies studied first the powerful rays, similar to X-rays, given off by the element uranium. They called the process radioactivity. Then they began to experiment with a mineral called pitchblende, whose radioactivity appeared to be far greater than that of uranium. This led to the discovery of a new radioactive element that they named polonium after the country of Marie's birth. Later, as a result of their research, another new element, this time called radium, was found producing radio-active waves of far greater strength. Even the birth of their two daughters, Irene and Eve in 1897 and 1904, did not interrupt their experiments. They used most of their money to pay for equipment and materials, did most of their work in a draughty, damp shed and suffered burns and illness because of the toxic chemicals they handled in their experiments. In recognition of their major discoveries, they were awarded one of science's top prizes, the Nobel Prize for Physics, in 1903. They shared the honour with French scientist Henri Becquerel, who had also been working on radioactivity at the same time.

But then suddenly disaster struck. One day the following year as Pierre crossed a busy street in Paris, he was knocked down and killed by a heavily loaded horse-drawn cart. Marie was devastated to have lost both her husband and her work partner. She confided in her diary that she was finding it difficult to carry on. 'How can I continue to work in a laboratory where I never thought I would have to live without you?'she wrote.

It was a major turning-point in her life. From then on she devoted even more of her time and energy to completing the scientific work they had started together. In 1906 she was appointed to the professorship that had been left by her husband's death and became the first woman to teach at the Sorbonne. She published her findings on radioactivity in 1910 and the following year was awarded a second Nobel Prize, this time in chemistry, for achieving the isolation of pure radium. By 1914 Marie had supervised the completion of the research laboratories at the newly built Institute of Radium in Paris, and during the First World War she worked with her daughter Irene to develop the use of radioactivity in the field of medicine.

In later life, Marie continued to extend the medical applications of the radioactive substances she had discovered. The word 'curie' came into the language as a unit for measuring radioactivity. Marie was able to travel the world lecturing and receiving medals, degrees and other honours. Wherever she went she used her influence to raise money for scientific research.

This incredible woman also wrote these words: 'One never notices what has been done; one can only see what remains to be done.' She died from a blood complaint in 1934 at the age of sixty-seven – killed by poison from the very substances she had struggled for so long to understand and which now can do so much good in the treatment of diseases like cancer.

MATERIAL WORLD

Make the children aware of the wide range of materials that exist in our world today by mounting a number of displays inside the classroom. These could each concentrate on a single material like wood, plastic, metal or fabric. Or they could show how many different materials are used in making the things we see and use every day, like a selection of different containers, for example. Encourage careful observation by making hand lenses and a microscope available so that children can examine in close-up how the materials are made up.

Begin to classify the materials by asking key questions.

- Which ones are natural and which are hand-made?
- Which ones would go well together and which might need to be kept apart?
- Which ones are alike and which are different?
- Does the material always come in the same colour?

  One way of heightening children's awareness is to put an object inside a sealed bag. One child should put their hands into the bag to feel the object while the other members of a small group should ask questions that the feeler has to answer carefully.

- Does it feel hard or soft?
- Is it pointed or round?
- What sort of texture does it have?
- Is it flexible or is it impossible to bend?
- Does it feel smooth and shiny like metal?
- Is it long and thin or short and fat?

  It is essential that children begin to relate materials to their uses and to realise that the way in which they are used usually depends on their properties.

- Why is so much wood used in making doors and furniture?
- Why is clear plastic often used in shops for wrapping things?
- Why do we use glass in windows?
- Why do we have more coins than notes in our money system?
- Why are tyres made out of rubber?
- Why is wool such a good material for keeping us warm?

  Questions like these should encourage the children to carry out tests on materials in order to check out their theories. See if they can devise their own investigations and make predictions before they start.

- How will they make the test fair and what measurements are they going to need to carry out?
- What would be the most appropriate form for recording their findings?
- What conclusions might they draw at the end and how will these be communicated to others?

One possible investigation would be to test the strength of carrier bags that are provided by major supermarkets for carrying goods home.

- What materials are used to make them?
- How are the materials used joined together?
- What would be the fairest way of seeing how effective these materials are?

Details of how to set this up are given on the photocopiable sheet *Happy shopper*? Or children could find out which materials are best for mopping up spillage in the home. If the test is to be fair, it will be important that the same amount of water is spilt each time and that the same sized piece of material is used for each spillage. How the water will be mopped up is also vital and some system of accurate measuring will be needed to ascertain how much water has been collected (see Figure 6.1).

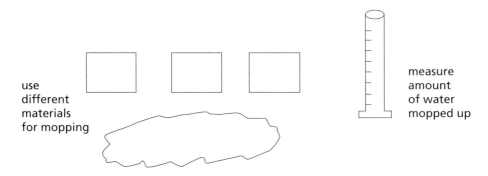

use
different
materials
for mopping

measure
amount
of water
mopped up

● **Figure 6.1:** The mop-up test

Solids, liquids and gases

No examination of materials would be complete without taking the opportunity to establish the fundamental differences between a solid, a liquid and a gas and how their characteristics vary because of the way in which their particles are bound together.

Because the particles in solids are held closely together, they cannot move around each other. For this reason solids have a definite shape although they do not always have to be hard and can come in powder form like flour. Soft solids can also have their shape changed through pressing. In liquids, the particles are close to each other but the forces holding them are not as strong as in solids so they tend to move around. The shape of a liquid will be determined by the kind of container it is in; when it is poured it will spread out. The particles in gases always move around quickly in all directions. The forces binding them are very weak so gases are able to spread and flow. This is the reason why gases have no fixed shape and why they will keep on spreading out until they completely fill the space they are contained in.

Water is often a good starting place because it is able to exist in all three of these states. Show the children that water is a liquid as it comes from the tap, when frozen it becomes solid and after heating it becomes a gas (Figure 6.2). Present groups with safe materials that have to be classified into the three states. Then narrow it down to pairs of materials and ask the children to identify similarities and differences. Get them to compare two hard solids, for example, like metal and wood. Then try something hard with something soft, like stone and Plasticine. Move on to contrast thinner liquids and thicker liquids like lemonade and fruit juice and a transparent solid like plastic sheeting with a transparent liquid like water. In their findings encourage children to avoid using blanket descriptions and generalisations. There is a need to be specific. All solids are not hard to the touch, for example, and not all gases are colourless. All liquids may not have water in them and an empty container is not really empty. They should be aware that solids with very small particles can often behave like liquids when they are poured. Get them to consider whether a material like sponge should be classified as a solid and a gas because it contains air between the particles.

| liquid | solid as ice | gas as steam |

● **Figure 6.2:** Three states of water

Increasing the children's understanding of gases at primary school level is much more difficult for safety reasons. But they can be shown where the gases in the air work in conjunction with liquids through bubbles in soapy water and the rising gas bubbles visible inside a gently shaken soft drinks bottle. They will appreciate that a solid can also control the extent to which gases spread, as this happens when we blow up a balloon or inflate a bicycle tyre. Use secondary sources to highlight the uses of some other gases. Talk about how natural gas is used to power things in the home. Why does a smell have to be added to it? Think about gases that keep up a hot-air balloon, what fire-fighters breathe when they go into a smoke-filled room, and why gases emitted from vehicle exhaust pipes and factory chimneys cause pollution (Figure 6.3).

● **Figure 6.3:** Pollution gases released into the air

Separating and changing materials

Much can be learnt about different materials and their properties by devising ways in which materials can be separated. Some methods are more obvious than others but are they always successful? Children could use a sieve to separate pebbles from rice, for example, but how effective would the sieve be for a mixture of sand and flour (Figure 6.4)? Could they suggest alternative strategies in this case? Talk about how recycling plants separate different types of metal using giant magnets and how useful this might be for separating out steel and aluminium cans. Filtering is in many ways just a more refined version of sieving and experiments using this system can be set up easily in the classroom. Figure 6.5 shows how to construct a simple filtering device that can be used to purify water. Here the water is filtered through gravel, sand and cotton wool and should reach the base of the container much cleaner than when it went in. Ask the children to think of other ways in which separation could take place.

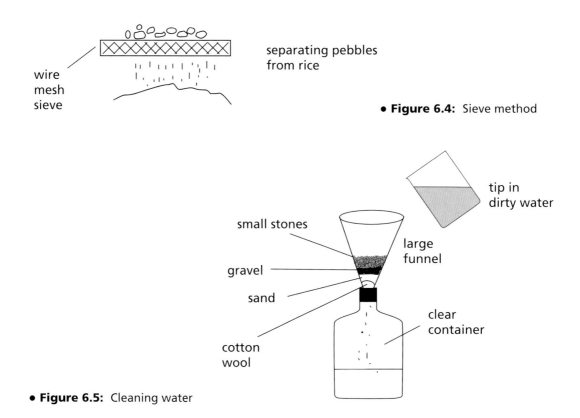

• **Figure 6.4:** Sieve method

• **Figure 6.5:** Cleaning water

Heat butter in a pan ready for cooking, put ice into a drink or turn hot air on to a frosted windscreen: it is not difficult to see that materials are changing their state all around us. Sometimes these changes are reversible while at other times or with other materials they are not.

Heating and cooling are perhaps the most common ways in which the states of materials are changed. Get children to consider and predict what might happen when certain materials are heated and whether they think it would be possible to get back the original material. Melt chocolate or butter to see what happens to it. Why and how do we try to keep materials like this at a low temperature? Discuss with the children why hot water is needed to make jelly and why a plastic bottle filled with water and placed in a freezer overnight will show signs of cracking the next day (Figure 6.6).

plastic bottle of
water from freezer

● **Figure 6.6:** Expanding bottle

Many children are under the impression that when a material dissolves in water it disappears. It is, of course, still present even though it may not easily be seen. Add a range of materials to cold water and observe what happens. Try sugar, salt, sand, cooking oil, coffee and tea. Tabulate the results.

● How can we tell that the material has dissolved?
● Is the amount of the material used important?
● Does it reach a saturation point?
● What do we mean by the term 'saturated solution'?
● Why has the material dissolved?
● Is it possible to get it back again?
● Could another liquid have been used instead of water?
● Is there any way of making the material dissolve faster?

Then compare how much of certain materials will dissolve in a given amount of water. Leave solutions for a few days and observe what happens to them. Have changes taken place? Why have they occurred?

Evaporation and condensation are key areas that also need to be considered within this theme. Talk to children about what happens when puddles in the playground start to dry out after a storm of rain and when wet washing is hung out to dry (Figure 6.7). Find the best drying places within the school grounds.

where is
the best
drying place?

● **Figure 6.7:** Wet washing

● What are the best drying conditions?
● What happens to the water, does it just vanish?

Leave the same amounts of water in differently-shaped containers on the classroom windowsills and see which ones will evaporate quickest. Show children that evaporation can be used to get dissolved substances back again by leaving out a saucer of salty water. Demonstrate how water evaporates when heated and then show the steam condensing once it hits a cold surface (Figure 6.9). Talk about the problems caused by condensation in the kitchen and bathroom. Why does it happen and how can it be prevented? Look at the part played by evaporation and condensation in the water cycle. A chance to develop this further is given on the photocopiable sheet *The water cycle.*

● **Figure 6.8:** From which container does water evaporate most quickly?

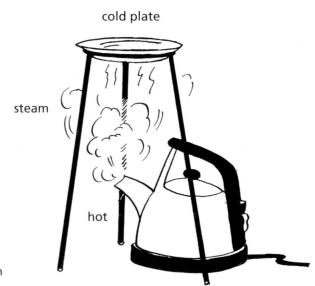

● **Figure 6.9:** Evaporation/condensation

SUPPORT

Keep experiments simple to make sure that the children are not overloaded with too many complex tasks. Spend a lot of time consolidating children's understanding of the concept of solid, liquid and gas. When comparisons are being made between materials, limit them to just two. Discuss predictions before investigations are carried out. Stress the importance of careful observation. Make sure scales on measuring devices are simple and easy to read. Provide key questions that children have to answer when they are expressing their findings. Reinforce important safety rules when materials are being used.

EXTENSION

Provide children with details of the basic concepts being investigated and ask them to devise their own tests to check them out. Check children's investigation plans to ensure they are safe to use. Stress the importance of fair testing if reliable and accurate results are to be obtained. Some tests may need to be repeated. Make sure appropriate measurements are taken. At the end of testing, ask children to draw their own conclusions. They should be able to communicate the outcomes effectively to other groups of children or the whole class in a variety of ways.

KEY VOCABULARY

Material, chemical, substance, solid, liquid, gas, natural, man-made, synthetic, hard, soft, thick, thin, clear, powder, particle, bend, stretch, melt, freeze, solidify, dissolve, solution, saturated, filter, sieve, purify, air, carbon dioxide, oxygen, helium, bubble, colourless, odourless, state, change of state, separate, reversible, irreversible, permanent, temporary, heat, temperature, cool, mixture, pure, condense, evaporate, condensation, evaporation, water cycle.

RESOURCES

Range of measuring jugs, cups and cylinders, wide range of different containers from saucers to large plastic bottles, scoops, collection of solids, liquids, powders for testing purposes, hand lenses, magnifying glasses, microscope, large bag, carrier bags, weights, pictures of items that use/contain gas, sieves, funnels, filter paper, soil, gravel and sand, cotton wool, range of fabrics and papers for mopping up experiment, supplies of water, ice cubes, kettle, heat source (e.g. hot plate) – both of these last two for use by the teacher only – magnets, thermometers, timers, fizzy drinks, washing-up liquid, balloons, bicycle tyre, sponge, the photocopiable sheets *Happy shopper* and *The water cycle*.

NATIONAL CURRICULUM LINKS

Key Stage 2 Science

- Sc 1 Scientific enquiry: 1 Ideas and evidence in science. 2 Investigative skills.
- Sc 3 Materials and their properties: 1 grouping and classifying materials – pupils should be taught (a) to compare everyday materials and objects on the basis of their material properties and to relate these properties to everyday uses of the materials; (e) to recognise differences between solids, liquids and gases, in terms of ease of flow and

maintenance of shape and volume. 2 Changing materials – pupils should be taught (a) to describe changes that occur when materials are mixed; (b) to describe changes that occur when materials are heated or cooled; (c) that temperature is a measure of how hot or cold things are; (d) about reversible changes including dissolving, melting, boiling, condensing, freezing and evaporating; (e) the part played by evaporation and condensation in the water cycle; (f) that non-reversible changes result in the formation of new materials that may be useful; (g) that burning materials results in the formation of new materials and that this change is not usually reversible. 3 Separating mixtures of materials – pupils should be taught (a) how to separate solid particles of different sizes by sieving; (b) that some solids dissolve in water to give solutions but some do not; (c) how to separate insoluble solids from liquids by filtering; (d) how to recover dissolved solids by evaporating the liquid from the solution; (e) to use knowledge of solids, liquids and gases to decide how mixtures might be separated.

Key Stage 2 Design and technology

● Knowledge and understanding of materials and components: pupils should be taught (a) how the working characteristics of materials affect the ways they are used; (b) how materials can be combined and mixed to create more useful properties.

ICT suggestions

Word processing for reports of investigations; use of database for work on materials, e.g. to record their properties.

Collect some carrier bags like the kind given away by supermarkets.
Go for variety – different sizes, styles and handles.

- What qualities would you be looking for?
- List any ways in which the bags are different.
- Test the strength of the bags carefully by using large tins of baked beans. Make sure the test is fair.
- Record your results in the chart:

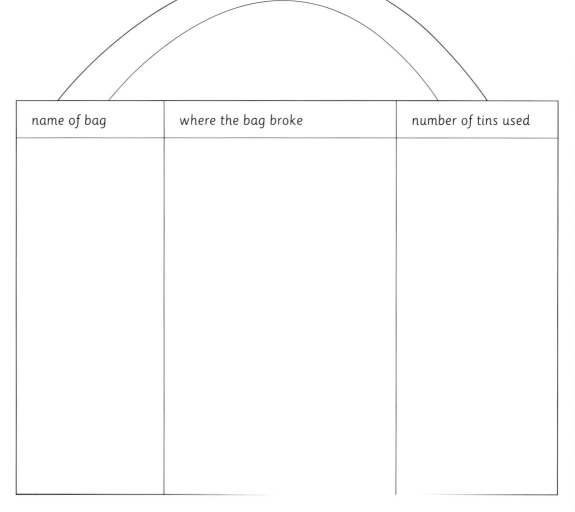

name of bag	where the bag broke	number of tins used

- What qualities did the best bag have?

- Research the meaning of the term 'water cycle'.
- Turn this sheet on its side and inside the box draw a diagram to illustrate the water cycle.
- Label the diagram using these key words.

Make sure they are placed in the correct position.

sun	river	cloud	sea	hill	rain
	evaporation		condensation		

The water cycle

7
Louis Pasteur
Protecting our bodies

Many famous scientists receive honours and rewards because of the contribution they have made during their lives, but few achieve something so significant that their name becomes part of the language.

Pasteurisation, the word given to the process in which milk is heated to a high temperature and pressure in order to kill any remaining germs, takes its name from Louis Pasteur. This dedicated French chemist not only investigated the causes of illness and disease, but also spent most of his working life searching for ways in which they might be prevented.

Pasteur, who was born in 1822, started experimenting at a time when people had no clear idea of how disease and infection were spread. Through careful research and testing with micro-organisms or microbes, he was able to show how these living things were passed on through water, air and food. He became convinced that these tiny creatures – so small most of them could not be seen by the naked eye – were the causes of disease, and that if ways of controlling them could be found, the health of people and animals would be greatly improved.

The son of a poor tanner who prepared animal skins for the leather industry, Pasteur grew up in a small village in the Jura Mountains close to France's frontier with Switzerland. He was not generally a good scholar but became fascinated by science while he was still at school. It was one of his early teachers who encouraged his interest in chemistry. He qualified as a doctor in Paris and, after a time spent in teaching and research in both Dijon and Strasbourg, he moved in 1854 to the University of Lille in northern France, where he was appointed professor of chemistry and head of the science department.

Throughout his career, Pasteur was someone who liked to use his expertise to solve practical problems. At various times during his life he worked with the brewing industry to find out why beer and wine sometimes went sour and became undrinkable. This was causing a number of economic difficulties in France. The most common belief then was that decay was the result of a chemical process that was spontaneous. But Pasteur was able to show that it happened through living micro-organisms that were actually the cause rather than the outcome of the problem. He experimented with heat during the early stages of the wine fermentation process and this led to the development of pasteurisation – a method of preventing liquids such as milk from going bad.

He also tackled problems in the silkworm industry in France when it was plagued with germs that were killing the worms. By this time in 1865 Pasteur had become the director of scientific studies at the Ecole Normale in Paris. He proved conclusively that the disease-producing organisms were not only contagious but that they were being passed on through the eggs to the next generation of silkworms. Only by the careful production and selection of disease-free eggs was the industry saved from disaster.

But it was through his research work involving serious and fatal animal and human diseases, like anthrax and rabies, that Pasteur made perhaps his biggest break-throughs. It was he, and others trying to find a solution to the same problems like Edward Jenner and Benjamin Jesty, who developed the idea of vaccination or inoculation. Pasteur realised that if an animal or a person were given a small dose of the disease virus by means of an injection, it would help them develop immunity if the disease struck in a more serious form later. In one of his best-known cases, a ten-year-old boy was brought to him after being badly bitten by a rabid dog. The boy was given an inoculation of the rabies virus and after a period of treatment lasting ten days had fully recovered. Thousands of people have been treated in the same way since. The scientist who once rescued businesses was now saving people's lives.

As a result of Pasteur's research into rabies, a special hospital for treating the disease was opened in Paris in 1888. It also investigated the treatment of other dangerous illnesses like cholera, tuberculosis and smallpox. This was named the Pasteur Institute and it is still an important centre for the study of infectious diseases today.

By the time of his death in September 1895, Pasteur was a national hero in France. A simple, modest man, who remained a devout Roman Catholic all his life, he was given a state funeral in the Cathedral of Notre Dame in Paris and was buried in a tomb underneath the famous institute he had been instrumental in setting up.

TOO SMALL TO SEE

It was scientists like Pasteur and Jenner who were the first to put forward the idea that is now called the germ theory – that it is micro-organisms or microbes that cause illness, disease and decay.

Children often associate the word 'decay' with looking after their teeth and, in a topic of this kind, this is one of the best places to start. Remind children of how micro-organisms in the mouth cause tooth decay and explain that the way to keep teeth and gums healthy is not only through the things we eat but also through careful cleaning with brush and floss. Invite a dental hygienist or dental nurse into school to talk to the children. They will be able to organise some simple tests with disclosure tablets and plastic mirrors to check how effective the children's teeth-cleaning habits are as well as giving general advice (Figure 7.1).

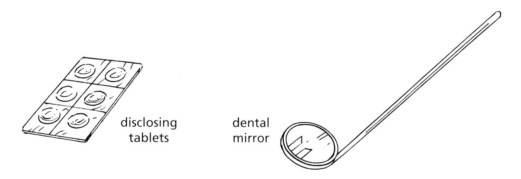

disclosing tablets   dental mirror

● **Figure 7.1:** Clean teeth

Carry out simple decay experiments in the class, showing examples of food going mouldy because of microbes. Foods like cheese and bread will both begin to show signs of mouldiness very quickly. Under adult supervision, leave some samples open to the air while placing others in sealed plastic bags and containers for the same period of time (Figure 7.2). This will help children appreciate all the effort people go to at home in order to keep food fresh. Discussion should also include the role played by airtight storage and refrigeration in food preservation and how our ancestors used to manage before the advent of the fridge and freezer. A study of food packaging will also reveal the amount of preservatives that are added to food items in order to keep them germ-free until they are used (Figure 7.3). Today we rely on chemical preservatives but more traditional methods of keeping food fresh like canning, smoking, pickling and salting are still used. The children will realise that, while the fungus-like mould that forms on food items exposed to the air is very visible, the bacteria that can cause serious

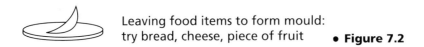
Leaving food items to form mould:
try bread, cheese, piece of fruit ● **Figure 7.2**

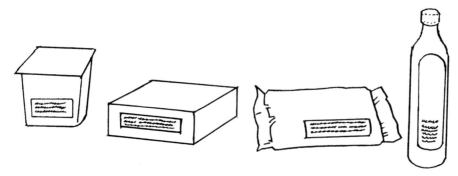

read food packaging for details of preservatives

● **Figure 7.3:** Food packaging

problems like food poisoning are not. In conjunction with research at home, ask them to devise a list of hygiene rules for the kitchen. This should include advice about the correct storage of food, e.g. raw and cooked meats should not be stored together, and the cleanliness of cooking utensils, equipment and work surfaces.

Ingredients	Utensils needed
200g plain flour	mixing board
25g margarine	teaspoon
1 level teaspoon salt	small basin
1 teaspoon of sugar	measuring jug
15g fresh yeast	baking sheet
125-150ml warm water	

● **Figure 7.4:** Bread recipe

To help provide some kind of balance, children should be made aware that micro-organisms can also be useful, particularly in the food industry. Discuss the part played by yeast in the bread-making process, for example, and let the children experiment with its use. A simple recipe for bread is given in Figure 7.4. Here the yeast reacts with the sugars in the dough to produce carbon dioxide gas. This helps the dough to rise and swell. It also accounts for the fact that bread contains so many air holes. Later, put a teaspoon of dried yeast into a bowl with a teaspoon of sugar and a cup of warm water. Watch what happens.

● Can the children explain this?
● Does the same thing happen without the sugar?
● What happens if the water is cold?
● Can the children set up some experiments to show that yeast is a micro-organism that lives, grows and reproduces?
● What does yeast need in order to do these things?

Children may be able to find out how yeast is used in brewing and wine-making and how micro-organisms are also utilised in other areas of food production, including the making of yoghurt and certain types of cheese.

Healthy diet

It should be made clear to the children from the start that the word 'diet' in this context is being used in its fullest sense. Here it means the range of food eaten by a person over a period of time and not a sudden curtailing of intake in order to achieve weight loss. There are also a number of other important factors to bear in mind here. On the question of a healthy diet always stress the need for balance – that is, eating a variety of foods in moderation. Remember that children of this age are at risk from eating disorders and that sensitivity should also be shown concerning religious, ethical and medical attitudes to food. Teachers should be mindful too of the children's own body images, especially if the class is talking about the weight of individuals.

Begin by asking the children to keep a diary of the foods they eat each day during a typical week. They can then start to classify food items according to a number of different criteria. Are they solids or liquids? Divide them into food items that come from animals and those that originate from plants (Figure 7.5). Which ones can be eaten raw and which ones have to be cooked first? Results charted on Venn diagrams

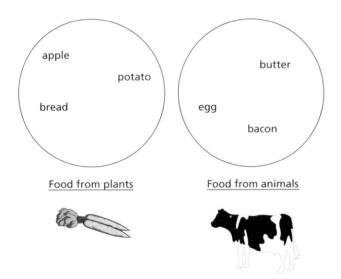

apple
potato
bread

Food from plants

butter
egg
bacon

Food from animals

● **Figure 7.5:** Plants/animals

will illustrate that some fit into both categories (Figure 7.6). How does the food change once it has been cooked? Then put items into food families like meat and fish, dairy produce, bread and cereals, and fruit and vegetables. Instead of using traditional block graphs to show the results of food surveys, ask the children to produce an appropriately named *pie* chart to indicate the breakdown of the foods they have eaten during a day or week (Figure 7.7). Think about which foods are needed for growth, which are required to provide energy for daily activity and which help to fend off illness and disease. Can children distinguish between what they like and what is good for them, bearing in mind that some dislikes may be based on allergies or medical conditions? Some children may be able to classify foods in more

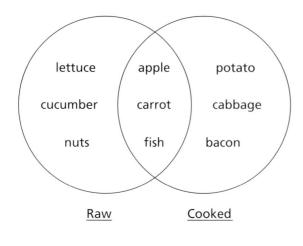

Raw   Cooked

• **Figure 7.6:** Raw, cooked

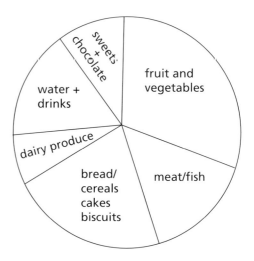

• **Figure 7.7:** Pie chart of food eaten in a day

technical terms like proteins, carbohydrates, fats and vitamins and minerals and know something about why we need regular supplies of each of these. One good way of producing a practical activity from the children's findings is to ask them, in small groups of four or five, to plan and make a three-course meal of starter, main course and dessert plus drinks for themselves. With an agreed budget to work to, they should plan the balanced meal that they intend to eat, make a supervised visit to the supermarket or shop to purchase their ingredients, prepare and cook the food themselves, wash up and tidy away and then evaluate the whole process.

Encourage children to monitor the food they eat and become more aware of the need for a balanced and healthy diet by introducing them to the traffic light system. Ask them to divide up the food they consume over a given period of time into three main areas. The 'green for go' section contains foods they can eat plenty of each day because it will be doing them good, e.g. fruit and vegetables. 'Amber for caution' will contain items that should be eaten in moderation, with intake kept under control. Crisps and bread might fit into here. The 'red for warning' category is for food substances that need to be monitored closely and should be eaten only in very limited amounts. Chocolate, cakes and biscuits would be included in this area. A chart for recording foods in these three categories is given on the photocopiable sheet *Traffic lights*. Large stores and supermarkets are increasingly producing their own literature on the subject of healthy eating and children may find this useful while involved in the 'traffic lights' decision-making process.

While on the subject of healthy eating, discuss with the class the use of well-known sayings about our eating habits to see if they might contain any elements of truth.

- Does an apple a day really keep the doctor away?
- Why do people say that eating carrots improves the eyesight?
- Why is water nicknamed 'Adam's ale'?
- It may work for Popeye but does spinach really give you extra strength?

Wrapping, sealing and protecting food items is important for safety, freshness and hygiene but it has its price. It will not have escaped children's notice that, of the rubbish that fills the nation's waste bins every week, about three-quarters is made up of discarded food packaging. Teach them the concept of the new three Rs – Reduce, Reuse and Recycle (Figure 7.8). Consider questions such as:

- Was the packaging really necessary in the first place?
- Could it be used again for something else?
- Could an environmentally-friendly alternative have been used?
- What would have been used in the past?
- If it cannot be reused, can this waste be recycled?

Reduce   –   the amount of packaging we have

Reuse   –   boxes and bags wherever we can

Recycle   –   especially paper, card, glass, metal

- **Figure 7.8:** The three Rs

The photocopiable sheet *Save it!* encourages children to look carefully at food packaging. Once they have decided what materials have been used in its manufacture, they will need to find out where and how it might be recycled.

Harmful effects

Just as children of this age become aware that certain foods may be detrimental to their health, they also begin to appreciate that there are other substances around that can have harmful effects. It is not true that poor health is totally attributable to an unhealthy lifestyle but, on the other hand, healthy living can help to protect people from becoming ill. Many of these issues will be dealt with in more detail in the school's personal, social and health education programme but this area of science also has its part to play.

Talk to the children about drugs – substances that in some way change the mental and physical state of the body. Remind them that, while most medicines are drugs, not all drugs are medicines. All drugs can be harmful if they are not used properly. Discuss how instructions must be followed carefully when medicines are taken and look at the rules that apply to the use of medicines within the school context. Consider the use and misuse of alcohol, the effects of taking in too much caffeine and the dangers of smoking.

Bring into the classroom posters and other forms of literature about the harmful effects of some substances to help focus discussion. There are many good videos that also present the arguments. Call in the health professionals to talk to the children and answer their questions. Use role-play situations to highlight how children come under the influence of peer group pressure and have to think things through for themselves in what is often a difficult decision-making process. Include the significant part played by the media in advertising the use of such things as alcohol and tobacco and the possible effects this has on people's thinking.

SUPPORT

Limit the number of healthy eating and food hygiene rules that the children are given so that they will take them in and remember them. Give guidance, e.g. prepared charts with group headings, when children are classifying foods within various families. Help with the use of charts, especially Venn diagrams and pie charts. Provide detailed lists of ingredients and recipes when children are cooking. Assist with the mathematical aspects of the cooking process, e.g. money for shopping and weighing and measuring ingredients. Provide support when sorting materials ready for recycling.

EXTENSION

Encourage children to do their own research for this topic. This might include the use of preservatives, food production, other micro-organisms that serve useful rather than harmful purposes and the meaning of technical words like protein, carbohydrate and vitamin. Ask them to devise and deliver their own questions when health professionals come into school to speak. Get them to make contact with the local authority to find out more about the amount of waste that is recycled in the area and what facilities are provided for ordinary members of the public to do this.

KEY VOCABULARY

Germ, bacteria, virus, micro-organism, microbe, decay, hygiene, health, mould, fungus, fungi, airtight, refrigeration, fridge, freezer, package, preservative, additive, raw, cooked, dough, yeast, sugar, starch, carbon dioxide, diet, solid, liquid, animal, plant, meat, fish, cereal, dairy produce, fruit, vegetable, growth, energy, disease, illness, ailment, allergy, protein, carbohydrate, fat, vitamin, mineral, balanced meal, menu, ingredients, recipe, reduce, reuse, recycle, environmentally friendly, material, manufacture, drug, substance, medicine, alcohol, tobacco, smoke, peer group, media, advertise.

NATIONAL CURRICULUM LINKS

Key Stage 2 Science

- Sc 1 Scientific enquiry: 1 Ideas and evidence in science. 2 Investigative skills.
- Sc 2 Life processes and living things. 2 Humans and other animals – pupils should be taught (a) about the function and care of teeth; (b) about the need for food for activity and growth and about the importance of an adequate and varied diet for health; (g) about the effects on the human body of tobacco, alcohol and other drugs and how these relate to their personal health. 5 Living things in their environment – pupils should be taught (f) that micro-organisms are living organisms that are often too small to be seen and that they may be beneficial or harmful.
- Sc 3 Materials and their properties: 1 Grouping and classifying materials – pupils should be taught (a) to compare everyday materials and objects on the basis of their material properties and to relate these properties to everyday uses of the materials.

Key Stage 2 Design and technology

- Developing, planning and communicating ideas.
- Working with tools, equipment, materials and components to make quality products: pupils should be taught to (f) follow safe procedures for food safety and hygiene.
- Evaluating processes and products.
- Knowledge and understanding of materials and components: pupils should be taught (a) how the working characteristics of materials affect the way they are used.
- Breadth of study: during the key stage, pupils should be taught the knowledge, skills and understanding through (c) designing and making assignments using a range of materials including food.

ICT suggestions

Word processing for reports of investigations; use of databases for classifying types of food, etc.

- Make a list of all the food you ate yesterday. Include drinks as well.
- Now sort the foods to fit into the traffic lights grid below.
  You can draw some pictures to illustrate your writing if you want to.

| Red for danger

Eat little of these	List/draw the food items here
Amber for caution

Eat moderate amounts | |
| Green for go

Eat plenty of these | |

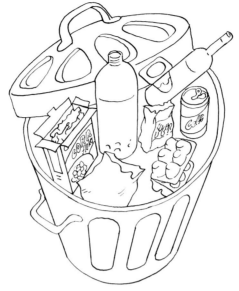

• List everything you can see in the rubbish bin

• Then complete the table below

• Find out about local recycling arrangements

Item	Material from which it is made	How it can be recycled

8
Galileo Galilei
Reaching for the stars

Many scientists throughout history have had to struggle hard against rivals and critics to get their views and theories accepted, but few have been threatened with imprisonment or torture if they failed to renounce their opinions.

The Italian scientist Galileo put forward ideas that were so radical in the seventeenth century that he alienated the Roman Catholic Church which kept him under closely supervised house arrest for the last ten years of his life. The pressure was so great that finally he was forced to say that his findings were wrong, even though he knew them to be correct. His final book, completed in 1639 with the help of colleagues, was smuggled from Italy to Holland for publication, as Galileo's friends were afraid that the information in it would lead to his arrest and possible execution.

The oldest of seven children, Galileo, who is usually known by just his first name even though he had two like everyone else, was born in the Italian city of Pisa in 1564. His father, who came from a noble family but worked as a musician and scholar, became particularly interested in the sounds produced by stringed instruments. Educated first at home by a tutor and then in a local monastery by the monks, Galileo later became a student of the University of Pisa. He started to study medicine but soon realised his interests lay elsewhere. He was nicknamed the 'wrangler' because of his habit of arguing with his teachers – often to make them look foolish – and it was not long before he switched to the study of mathematics.

By 1589 he had become professor of mathematics at his home town university and three years later moved to another Italian city, Padua, to take up a similar position there. In 1610 he was appointed chief mathematician to the Grand Duke of Tuscany. By then his discoveries were beginning to be well known but he was also making enemies in very influential positions.

The trouble started when Galileo began investigations into ideas about the first practical telescope. These had been put forward by a Dutch optician named Hans Lippershey. By 1592, with very little information to go on, Galileo had designed and built a powerful astronomical viewing device of his own. Through this he was able to view sunspots, the four main satellites of Jupiter, the mountains and craters of the Moon and the appearance of Venus going through its phases. It was this last observation, among others, that convinced him that the planets, including the Earth, were in fact orbiting the Sun and not the other way around, as most scientists believed at the time. In expressing this opinion he strongly supported the claims of the Polish monk, Nicholas Copernicus, who had made these suggestions many years earlier. Copernicus had published his beliefs in 1543, but the Roman Catholic Church had banned his book on the grounds that the idea that the Earth was not the centre of the universe went against the teachings of the Bible.

The church authorities were particularly concerned about the work Galileo was doing for two main reasons: first because he was a popular figure in Italy; and secondly because he wrote up his ideas and concepts in ordinary simple Italian and not the academic language of the time, which was Latin. Starting in 1611, Galileo was given a series of warnings by the Church that he should not continue to put forward his revolutionary views on the universe. He took little notice and the crisis point was reached in 1633 – a year after the publication of his famous book *Dialogue Concerning the Two Chief World Systems*. For eighteen days the Church's strict legal experts, often accurately referred to as The Inquisition, interrogated Galileo. To avoid possible torture and then imprisonment he agreed to change his views in his next book and publicly stated on oath that what he had previously written was wrong. Despite these assurances and the fact that his health was poor, the Church imprisoned him and he was placed under house arrest in his villa near Florence until his death at the age of seventy-seven in 1642.

Galileo is best known for his work in astronomy that changed people's concept of the universe, but he was an accomplished scientist in a number of other fields. He made important discoveries on the acceleration and movement of objects, did pioneering work on the use of pendulums in time-keeping devices and invented a water pump, a compass and a thermometer. In October 1989 the spacecraft launched by the space shuttle Atlantis on a six-year journey to explore Jupiter was named Galileo in honour of one of Italy's most famous sons.

THE EARTH AND BEYOND

Even during the Middle Ages there were explorers like Christopher Columbus, for example, who believed the Earth was round and not flat. But it is only in the last fifty years or so, since the advent of efficient spacecraft and improved photography, that pictures have confirmed what everyone believed to be true about the shape of the other planets in the solar system.

A good starting point is to ask the children, without help, to draw what they think the solar system looks like showing as much detail about layout and size as possible. Once these views have been examined and discussed, planning what needs to be covered will be simpler. Whatever is decided, this is a topic in which secondary sources are vital. Mount large displays in the classroom that will give the children as much information as possible about our neighbouring planets, their size, distance from the Earth and from each other, topological features and satellites. The large distances and sizes that are involved here often fascinate children and much discussion will be needed even to begin to appreciate the vastness of space. As well as collecting important statistics, children may also want to draw up a profile of their favourite planet. A data collection grid that could be used to do this is shown in Figure 8.1. Talk about round-the-world yacht races and the recent circumnavigation of the globe by hot-air balloon to reinforce the concept of the Earth being a sphere. Stress key pieces of information like the fact that the Earth takes 365¼ days to orbit the Sun, and the Moon goes around the Earth in about twenty-eight days. It is also important that children understand that it is the Sun that stays still and the Earth that moves and that the planet we live on also spins on its axis once every twenty four hours.

Make a full and accurate model of the solar system with small groups of children each taking responsibility for a different planet. This will help to correct popular misconceptions that the planets are quite close together and that they are alike in size. Use a balloon, blown up to the correct size, or a golf, table tennis or tennis ball as the central core for each planet, then build up the shape and size with papier mache. The advantage of using a balloon is that it can be popped once the modelling is complete. Create the colours of the planets' surfaces by laying on tissue paper or paint. Saturn's rings could be made from card, fixed to thin, shaped wire for stability. Display the model in such a way that it demonstrates the relative distances between the planets and between each planet and the Sun. This could be done down a long corridor or outside on the playground. Display a short piece of factual information about each planet alongside. Think about key questions.

- Which planets are close to each other?
- Which are similar in size?
- Which groups make up the inner planets and the outer planets?
- Why are they called this?

Planet factfile	
Name:	
Size:	
Distance from Sun:	
Surface:	
Atmosphere:	
Moons:	
Rings:	
Day length:	
Time to go round Sun:	
Illustration:	

Figure 8.1: Planet data collection grid

There are other practical tasks that can be set up and carried out easily to provide information and help underline concepts. Explore the apparent movement of the Sun across the sky each day from its rising in the east to its setting in the west by using a shadow stick. On a sunny day set up a vertical stick in a quiet part of the school grounds and use pegs to mark the position and the length of the shadow made each hour between nine o'clock in the morning and three o'clock in the afternoon (Figure

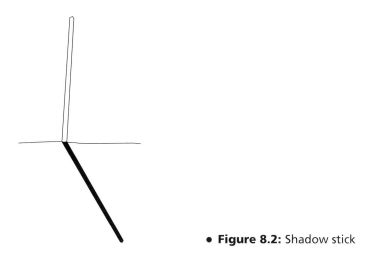

● **Figure 8.2:** Shadow stick

8.2). Carried out at different times of the year, this will also help the children to begin to understand seasonal variations in the position of the Earth in relation to the Sun. Remind the children constantly during this topic that it is dangerous to look at the Sun even if through sunglasses. Use a strong light source like a torch or a lamp and a model globe in a darkened room to demonstrate how night and day result from the Earth's spinning on its axis (Figure 8.3). Collect times of sunrise and sunset from local newspapers and talk about how seasonal differences might affect how light it is when children are going to and from school at different times of the year. Discuss the reasons why we change our clocks twice a year in this country. The photo-copiable sheet *Moon view* provides a chart that can be used by the children to record the phases of the Moon throughout the period of a month as it orbits the Earth. These phases are illustrated in Figure 8.4. Cloudless skies and good weather will be needed

● **Figure 8.3:** Night and day

new moon

crescent

quarter moon

gibbous

full moon

● **Figure 8.4:** Phases of the moon

for complete coverage, but any gaps that occur can be filled in by using details shown in the newspapers. Make sure the children understand that the Moon turns, so that the same side always faces the Earth and that moonlight is in fact light reflected from the Sun. Talk about the features of the Moon's landscape that are visible with the naked eye. Some of the hollows and depressions are still called seas – the name given to them by Galileo – even though we now know the surface is completely free of water.

Journey into space

While children should be encouraged to use their imaginations when designing and making their own model spacecraft, a look at pictures and models will give them a better idea of construction.

● Which parts are essential to the space vehicle?
● What additional parts might be needed?
● How does the craft move through space?

Insist that older children devise and make their own 3D shapes from nets rather than adapting boxes once used for packaging. Consider and test ways in which materials can be joined together, especially those with curved surfaces (Figure 8.5). Joining cylinders to flat surfaces is always a problem. Experiment with different kinds of glue to see which does the best job. Encourage the inclusion of moving parts (see Figure 8.6) and stress the importance of finishing off models attractively. If plastics are being used, paint will need additives like PVA glue to make it adhere. It may be possible to include lights so some revision of different circuits and switches may be needed.

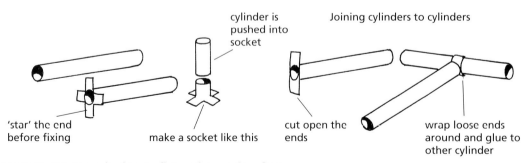

cylinder is pushed into socket

Joining cylinders to cylinders

'star' the end before fixing

make a socket like this

cut open the ends

wrap loose ends around and glue to other cylinder

● **Figure 8.5:** Joining cylinders to flat and curved surfaces

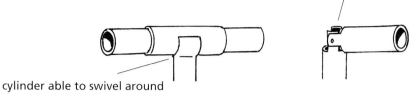

straw ends can be cut and pinned like this to make hinged corners

cylinder able to swivel around

● **Figure 8.6:** Moving parts

Allow the children plenty of scope. They could design and make a rocket, satellite, probe, shuttle or space station. Ask them to think about what shape it will be. In evaluating the finished product, get them to consider how much it differs from the original design.

● What changes had to be made and why?
● Were suitable materials chosen?
● Did they combine well?
● Were joins and fixtures both strong and tidy?
● Was the model finished off successfully?

There is also the chance within this topic to carry out pure design activities. Children could think about what the inside of a space station might look like. Details could be shown in cross-section, plan and side views.

● How would the living quarters be separated from the operational areas?
● What sort of beds would there be?
● Where would supplies of water come from?
● How would people move around inside if there was no gravity?

Or designs could be made of the type of spacesuit people would need to wear in space. It would need to be comfortable yet highly protective. How would the space traveller move, breathe and communicate?

Then give children the opportunity to plot the main events in the history of space exploration on the timeline given on the photocopiable sheet *Exploring space timeline*. Some key events of their own choice could also be added.

Beneath our feet

While studying the Earth and other planets in the solar system, also take time to examine the rocks and soils that lie just beneath our feet.

Children often fail to realise that rocks are all around us. We see them clearly in cliffs, quarries, mountains and buildings but they are, of course, everywhere under the ground. Rocks are used for purposes that suit their particular qualities and characteristics. Marble is often found inside buildings because it is decorative and can be polished, limestone is used on the outside of buildings because it is easy to shape and carve while granite takes on tougher jobs because of its strength. Ask the children to think about what the school is made of and why different materials are used in different parts of the building. If the building is old it may have stone walls and slate roofs while newer ones may be made of bricks, tiles and concrete. All of these materials come from rocks, but the children may need help to understand that bricks and tiles are baked clay and that concrete is made from a mixture of cement, sand and gravel.

Gather together a collection of rocks for the children to look at. Make it as varied as possible but it will be more interesting and relevant if the children know that some of the samples form part of the local geology. There should at least be representatives of the three main rocks groups – igneous, sedimentary and metamorphic. Sort the specimens into groups according to their colour, shape, weight, pattern and texture. Clue cards that have to be matched to the correct sample make a good introduction. Examine each sample through a hand lens to see how the particles are made up.

- Can any crystals be seen?
- Is it possible to see small stones or sand?
- Is it made up of tightly fitting layers like slate?
- Can the children find ways of calculating the volume and mass of the rocks?

The largest in size need not necessarily be the heaviest. Ask them to explain why. Carry out some simple but fair tests using the samples. Try scratching and rubbing to see if the rock will wear away. Is it possible to arrange the rocks in order of hardness. In the nineteenth century, a German geologist, Friedrich Mohs, devised a scale of hardness for ten rocks. He found that each rock in the scale could scratch the ones below itself but the ones above were too hard to scratch. Weigh the rocks carefully and then immerse them in water overnight. Weigh them again. Which ones has the water permeated? How much water have they taken in? With care it may also be possible to test them with vinegar to see whether any of the samples contain calcite (calcium carbonate). Because vinegar is a weak acid it will react with the calcite to produce carbon dioxide. The fizzing that the children will be able to observe is the carbon dioxide being given off.

Also collect some soil samples from the local environment. Ask children from different parts of the neighbourhood to bring them in. Turn the samples out on to sheets of paper and let the children observe them through a magnifying lens. What is soil actually made up of? Note similarities and differences. Put each of the samples into clean water in separate containers, fix on the lids, shake them up and allow them to settle. How do the particles separate into different layers? How are the layers in each sample different?

SUPPORT

Guidance and help will need to be given when children are using reference books and the CD-Rom for gathering information about the solar system. Information will need to be simplified, word banks will be needed to help with spelling and factfiles of basic information required. Since very large numbers will often be involved in discussions about the planets, help will be needed with approximating, rounding off and scaling down. Enlist the help of parents and carers as some of the tasks, e.g. the Moon phases data collection chart, will need to be done outside school time. Give assistance with measuring, cutting, shaping, fixing and finishing off during model making.

EXTENSION

Insist that the children do as much of their own research as possible when they are finding out about the planets in the solar system. Encourage them to produce their own detailed planet profile, complete with accurate information. Spacecraft designs should be done in as much detail as possible before actual building starts. Plans, even though they may change as construction progresses, should contain drawings from several different viewpoints, lists of materials and other resources needed and some idea of the dimensions involved. Children should incorporate moving parts in their spacecraft models and may wish to include other extras like lighting systems. Expect children to make their own entries on the space exploration timeline once facts have been researched.

KEY VOCABULARY

Earth, Sun, Moon, solar system, telescope, planet, satellite, globe, circumnavigate, sphere, spherical, revolve, spin, orbit, rotate, axis, shadow, compass, north, south, east, west, sunrise, sunset, phase, hollow, depression, rocket, probe, shuttle, space station, cliff, quarry, mountain, marble, limestone, granite, slate, brick, concrete, cement, gravel, sand, geology, geologist, igneous, sedimentary, metamorphic, mass, volume, texture, particle, crystal, layer, immerse, permeate, absorbent, calcite, carbon dioxide.

RESOURCES

Pictures, charts, photographs of the solar system and spacecraft of various kinds, balloons, collections of small balls, glue, paper, water for papier mache, wire, sticks, compass, tape measures, globe, lamp or torch, newspapers, wood, cardboard, paper, plastic, scissors, glue, sticky tape for model making, technology tools, bulbs, batteries, materials for switches, collection of rock samples, hand lenses, water, vinegar, soil samples, large clear containers with lids, the photocopiable sheets *Moon view* and *Exploring space timeline*.

NATIONAL CURRICULUM LINKS

Key Stage 2 Science

- Sc 1 Scientific enquiry: 1 Ideas and evidence in science. 2 Investigative skills. Sc 3 Materials and their properties: 1 Grouping and classifying materials – pupils should be taught (d) to describe and group rocks and soils on the basis of their characteristics including appearance, texture and permeability.
- Sc 4 Physical processes: 4 The Earth and beyond – pupils should be taught (a) that the Sun, Earth and Moon are approximately spherical; (b) how the position of the Sun appears to change during the day, and how shadows change as this happens; (c) how day and night are related to the spin of the Earth on its own axis; (d) that the earth orbits the Sun once each year, and that the Moon takes approximately twenty-eight days to orbit the Earth.

Key Stage 2 Design and technology

- Developing, planning and communicating ideas.
- Working with tools, equipment and components to make quality products.
- Evaluating processes and products.
- Knowledge and understanding of materials and components.
- Breadth of study: during the key stage, pupils should be taught the knowledge, skills and understanding through (b) focused practical tasks that develop a range of techniques, skills, processes and knowledge; (c) designing and making assignments using a range of materials.

ICT suggestions

Word processing for reports of investigations; use of computer based reference materials for researching planets, etc.

MOON VIEW

Moon observation sheet: Draw a small picture of how the moon looks in the night sky each night for the next three weeks. Write 'too cloudy' if you cannot see it.

Date						
Observation						
Date						
Observation						
Date						
Observation						

Find out the answers to these questions: What gives the Moon its light? How long does it take to go around the Earth? Why can we sometimes see the Moon in the day? How big is the Moon? How far away from us is it? What are the phases of the moon called?

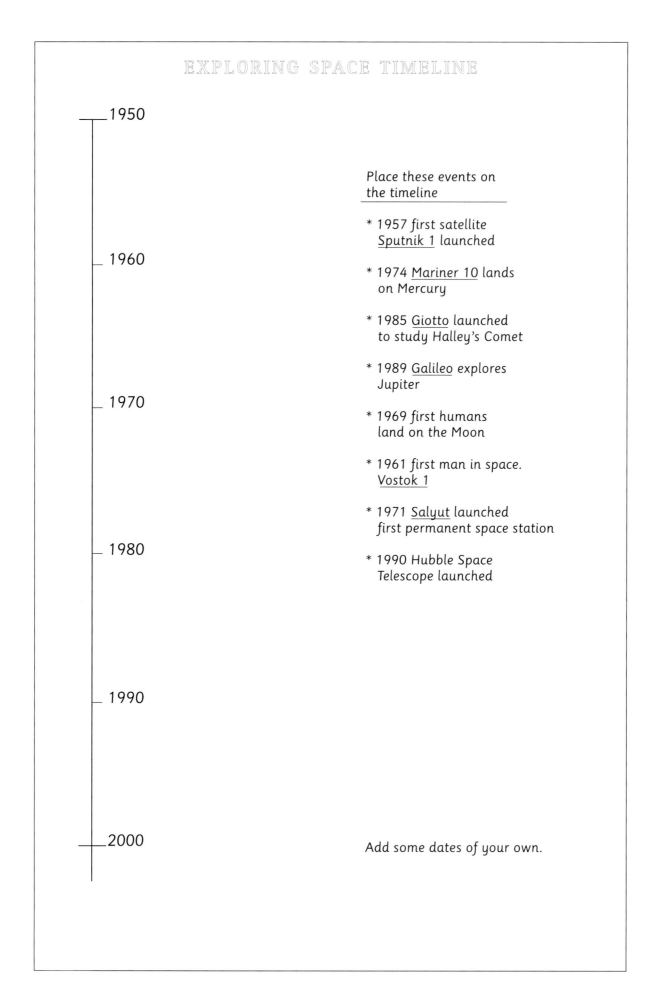

1950

1960

1970

1980

1990

2000

Place these events on
the timeline

* 1957 first satellite
  Sputnik 1 launched

* 1974 Mariner 10 lands
  on Mercury

* 1985 Giotto launched
  to study Halley's Comet

* 1989 Galileo explores
  Jupiter

* 1969 first humans
  land on the Moon

* 1961 first man in space.
  Vostok 1

* 1971 Salyut launched
  first permanent space station

* 1990 Hubble Space
  Telescope launched

Add some dates of your own.

9
Gregor Mendel
Watching the plants grow

Gardening is one of the most popular pastimes for many people in this country and there are those who spend hours each week tending their lawns, flowers and vegetables. But how dedicated would they be if they limited their activities to growing 30,000 plants of a single type and then studied them for nine years to see what developments took place?

This was the time-consuming and detailed task taken on by an Augustinian monk called Gregor Johann Mendel. His meticulous observations of the common garden pea not only revealed how characteristics develop in the plant world, but also helped us to understand those identifying features that make each human being an individual.

Mendel was born in a small village in the country we now call the Czech Republic, in 1822. He lived here with his family, who were poor farm workers looking after fruit trees for the local landowner, until 1843. Then, after leaving university because of lack of money, he joined an order of Augustinian monks in a monastery at Brno. He was ordained as a priest in 1847. Because the monks were a teaching order, Mendel was sent to the University of Vienna in Austria to gain his qualifications before returning to Brno to teach science in the local school.

It was here, on a small patch of the monastery garden, that Mendel combined his love of mathematics and his knowledge of plants to pursue his hobby: botanical research. For almost nine years, beginning in 1857, he grew peas in the garden and kept highly detailed records of what he was doing. His findings laid the foundations of the branch of science known today as genetics, the study of why offspring happen to inherit the characteristics of their parents.

Mendel wrapped up his plants to make sure they self-pollinated and could not be cross-pollinated by insects. This meant that their inherited features could only come from one parent. He saved seeds from each plant, planted them and studied what grew for each generation. Among other things, he noticed that dwarf plants produced only dwarf plants generation after generation while, of the tall plants, about one-third of them bred true. Of the rest some were tall and some were dwarf in the ratio of three to one. Later, when he crossed dwarf plants with true-breeding tall plants, he discovered the dwarf characteristics disappeared altogether. It was Mendel's work that showed that both parents pass on chemical instructions to their young. These instructions we now call genes. Some genes were more dominant or powerful and pushed weaker ones – known as recessive – into the background. The whole process by which genes were passed on from one generation to another is known today as heredity.

It is not really clear whether Mendel realised the importance of the work he had been doing. His discoveries were written up in several detailed papers that were read to the local scientific society but they appear to have made little impression outside the immediate area. He also wrote to Karl Wilhelm von Nageli, Germany's leading botanist, who was a professor at the University of Munich. But he showed little interest in the mathematical data that Mendel had collected and failed to share it with a wider audience. So often Mendel's work was seen by either botanists who did not understand mathematics or mathematicians who had no background in botany.

We now know that Mendel's findings on inherited characteristics can also be applied to the animal kingdom. Unfortunately, he did not have the opportunity to pursue his studies in this direction, as experimenting with the breeding of mice was not possible because of the strict rules concerning the use of animals in the monastery.

When Mendel was elected abbot or leader of the monastery, his experimental work with plants had to take second place, as he became more closely involved in the day-to-day administration of the order. He also began to take an interest in bee-keeping and other aspects of agriculture and this further limited his time. Towards the end of his life Mendel became caught up in the struggle with the Austrian government to lower the taxes paid by religious organisations and this too took him away from his studies.

Mendel died in 1884 at the age of sixty-two without ever knowing that later he would become extremely famous when his work was rediscovered at the beginning of the twentieth century. It was then that a number of different botanists, all working independently of each other, began to duplicate his research. Once his original papers had been uncovered they did not, to their credit, try to claim his findings as their own and that is why the laws of inheritance today are still known as Mendelian.

CONDITIONS FOR GROWTH

Almost wherever we look, plants surround us. They range from tiny organisms to mighty trees and are essentially the key to all life on earth. The giant sequoia trees of North America are the planet's oldest living things. Ask children to list down places where plants grow in their own local environment, from parks and gardens to rivers and fields. Think first about all the factors that plants have in common.

- Arc they usually green?
- Do they make food in the same way?
- Do they continue to grow throughout the whole of their lives?

Then try to divide the plants listed into groups or families of some kind. Start with a breakdown into flowering and non-flowering plants (some examples are given in Figure 9.1). Discuss how plants are suited to growing in particular areas and ask the children to suggest reasons why this might be. Is it connected to climatic conditions or are there other reasons? Using secondary sources, talk about plants in other parts of the world that have to be specially adapted in order to survive.

Flowering plants	Non-flowering plants
deciduous trees	fungi – mushrooms, moulds
grasses, cereals	mosses – lichens
daisy, buttercup	ferns
dandelion	coniferous trees: pines, firs

● **Figure 9.1:** Dividing plants into categories

- How do plants manage in desert regions, for example, where there is little rainfall?
- How do some combat the icy winds and low temperatures of high altitude?
- How do plants deal with the dampness and humidity found in jungles?
- How can some continue to thrive despite being saturated in salty water all the time?
- Why do some plants need other things to cling on to and why are others complete parasites?

A visit to any food shop or supermarket would help to emphasise the important part that plants play in our daily intake of food. Any examination of the vast quantities of fruits, vegetables, edible grasses, spices, herbs, seeds, nuts and berries that we consume should help children to realise just why we need plants to grow well (Figure 9.2).

Food item	Plant it comes from
bread	wheat – edible grass
milk	grass – eaten by cows
crisps	potato – sliced and fried

● **Figure 9.2:** Where does our food come from?

Set up experiments in the classroom that will help children to understand what conditions suit plants best if they are to flourish. Begin with something like mustard and cress seeds that will germinate quickly and show clear signs of growth within a short period of time. If results are to be both valid and reliable, it is vital in such experiments that testing is seen to be fair for all the seeds planted and that some do not gain an unfair advantage. Get children to organise their own investigation but suggest they try to isolate different factors at different times while keeping most factors constant. Use the same type and number of seeds in each growing position tried, for example. Plant them in the same soil and use the same containers. Give them equal amounts of water each day. It may be decided, of course, not to water some of the seeds as part of the experiment. Find a range of different locations to place the seeds. Try light situations like windowsills and others that are a complete contrast, like dark cupboards. Place a tray of seeds in a position known to remain warm and put others in the fridge. Monitor the seeds at regular intervals, observe their growth carefully and encourage children to describe in detail what they see.

● How long did they take to germinate?
● How high have the tiny plants grown?
● What colour are the leaves?
● Do they look strong or weak and spindly?

From their observations children should be able to produce a list of the conditions that the seeds needed in order to make them grow successfully.

Investigate further by using other plants and take full advantage of seasonal variations. Try small potted houseplants to see how they respond to different locations, varying amounts of water and feed. Remove some leaves to see what effect this might have on growth. Experiment in the summer months with flowering

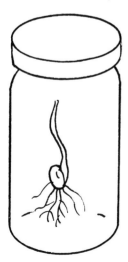

bedding plants like marigolds and keep detailed records and accurate measurements of their development. Grow broad or mung beans in clear containers where the growth of roots and shoots is visible (Figure 9.3). Plant bulbs in the autumn in pots, outside and in special jars where their root systems can be easily observed. Check regularly on them throughout the winter until they flower in the spring. Encourage the children to make regular observations on an outdoor plant, especially if the school has a wildlife area in the grounds. Choose something like thistle or dandelion that has a fairly short life cycle in the growing season. Record the plant's development with regular entries in some kind of log that tries to explain why changes have taken place and also predicts what might happen next.

● **Figure 9.3:** Growing bean in a glass jar

Doing its job

Use a commonly found flowering plant like the buttercup to stimulate children's thinking about the important job carried out by each of its parts. Careful dissection and the use of magnifying glasses and hand lenses will give the children good close-up views of different parts of the plant. Most should be able to label these parts while others will be able to explain the functions they perform in more detail (Figure 9.4).

● **Figure 9.4:** Buttercup to label

Talk about the dual role of the root system in anchoring the plant to the ground as well as drawing up vital water and minerals from the soil. Try to show children an example of a plant that has become 'pot bound' and get them to suggest what problems this might cause. Discuss how the stem links the roots to the rest of the plant as well as holding up the leaves and flowers to life-giving sunlight. It needs to be very strong in order to support the weight of the plant and stand up to the force of the wind. Look at the way in which the stalk helps to keep the leaves apart so they can produce the maximum amount of food. One easy way to follow the progress of moisture up through the plant is to place a head of celery in some water that has been coloured with red food colouring. Measure the amount of time it takes the 'redness' to work its way up through the stem until it begins to colour even the leaves at the top (Figure 9.5). Stress the importance of sunlight to growing plants by covering a small patch of grass with a large piece of metal or wood for several days.

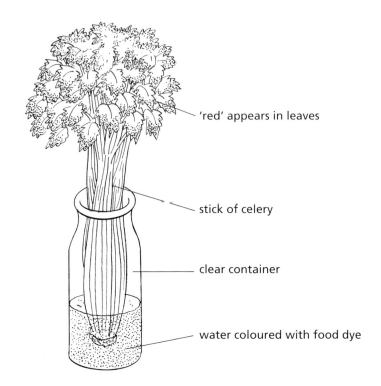

'red' appears in leaves

stick of celery

clear container

water coloured with food dye

● **Figure 9.5:** Celery

● What happens to the 'greenness' of the grass?
● Would the same thing happen for all plants?
● How long does it take to recover?

Life cycles

Consider the role of flowers in producing seeds for the next generation of plants. Many are brightly coloured to attract the insects needed for pollination but not all, especially some of the flowers produced by trees. Children should be able to identify and label the outer parts of the flower like the sepals and petals. They should know that the male part of the flower, called the *stamen*, produces the pollen and that the female part – the carpel – consists of an ovary that contains one or more ovules. It also has a long stalk or style and at the tip of this is the pollen receiving area called the stigma (see Figure 9.6). Distinguish between the two main methods of pollination. Self-pollination is where the transfer of pollen takes place within the same flower while cross-pollination occurs when pollen is taken from one flower to another of the same species. Sometimes the male and female organs are carried in separate flowers or even on different plants. Explain that most plants are pollinated by the wind or by insects and that seeds are formed when pollen fertilises the ovum.

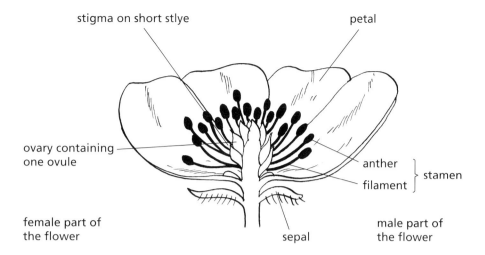

stigma on short stlye

petal

ovary containing
one ovule

anther

filament

stamen

female part of
the flower

sepal

male part of
the flower

● **Figure 9.6:** Parts of a flowering buttercup

Having produced a large number of seeds, the plant now needs to find a way of making them travel over as wide an area as possible. In some cases the mechanism for sending seeds away lies within the plant itself but usually some kind of agent is needed. During the autumn children should be encouraged to collect as many different seeds and fruits as they can. Ask the children to find different ways in which to classify them. Examine a number of key questions.

● Why does a plant need to produce so many seeds?
● Why is it better to get them as far away as possible from the parent plant?
● In what way are the seeds and fruits specially adapted to suit their form of dispersal?
● Who or what plays the most important part in moving the seeds about?

It may be possible to save some of the seeds for planting in the spring. This can either be done in pots or in marked plots in the school grounds. What conditions do they need to find in order to germinate successfully?

Talk about plants with stones and seeds inside brightly coloured fleshy fruit like cherries or blackberries that are attractive to birds and animals and how they are moved to new locations as they pass through the creatures' digestive systems. Nuts and acorns are buried by squirrels and often forgotten. Mention others, burdock and teasel for example, whose hooks help them hitch a ride on passing animals. Some trees, such as maple, sycamore and ash have winged fruits that spin while flowers like dandelion and thistle use feathery parachutes to transport the seeds around. The poppy scatters its seeds when a capsule at the top of a long thin stem sways in the breeze and some fruits in pods, like the gorse, explode in hot weather, throwing seeds in all directions. Can children find a plant that does not seem to have any seeds? Is it the wrong time of the year for it to produce seeds? Are the seeds too tiny to be seen? Is the plant too young to be producing seeds of its own? The main stages of the life cycle of a flowering plant are shown in Figure 9.7. The photocopiable sheet *Life cycle of the oak* shows the life cycle of a large plant – the oak tree – but the stages have been mixed up. Ask the children to cut them out and rearrange them in the correct order.

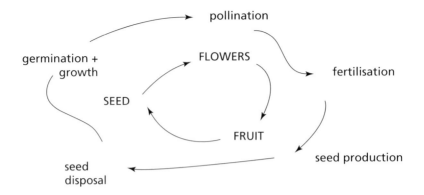

• **Figure 9.7:** Life cycle of flowering plant

Habitats and food chains

A large plant, like a tree for example, is not only a living organism in its own right, it also provides the habitat for many other plants and animals. If there is a large tree in the school grounds, encourage children to carry out their own investigation into who and what lives in and around it by carefully collecting samples. Remind the children that small creatures brought into the classroom for study should always be treated sensitively and returned to their habitat after study. Can they record their findings using some kind of key and are they able to classify the plants and animals they have found into appropriate families? Get them to think about the effect on plants and animals if habitats are suddenly changed or even removed. On the photocopiable sheet *Where is my home?* there is an illustration of a large tree and some of the living things that rely on it for life and so form its community. In discussion see if the children can link an animal's habitat directly to the food it eats. Can it live only in places that are a good source of its own chosen food and what other important conditions are necessary? Following further research, talk about the key words producer, consumer, decomposer, predator, prey, carnivore and herbivore in the context of food chains. Using some of the plants and animals collected in the habitat study, ask children to record their own food chains. They may be able to think of other examples. Can they establish what comes as the first stage in all food chains – even plants need to rely on the energy produced by the Sun. Some examples of food chains are given in Figure 9.8.

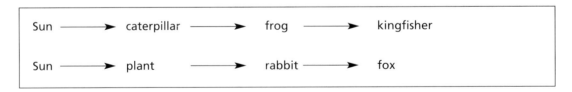

• **Figure 9.8:** Food chains

SUPPORT

Select pictures, charts and photographs with large labelled pictures and simple text when children are researching plant life. Prepare and explain the use of equipment when the children are carrying out the growing experiments. Provide clear lists of instructions with guided questions when experiments are being done. Help children to tabulate results of all practical work in a structured way. Assist with the collection and identification of mini-beasts when working on habitats. Provide examples of life cycles and food chains in the wrong order and ask children to rearrange them correctly.

EXTENSION

Expect children to carry out as much of their own research as possible using a range of reference sources including CD-Rom. Encourage children to suggest and collect the equipment they need for experiments with plants. Get them to suggest their own investigations into plant life based on a range of different criteria. Expect them to write up their findings in a detailed way with clear conclusions. Give them the names of certain plants and animals and see if they can locate the habitats where they can be found. Ask them to research their own examples of both life cycles and food chains.

KEY VOCABULARY

Gene, genetics, heredity, hereditary, botanist, biology, environment, habitat, flowering, non-flowering, desert, temperature, altitude, humidity, saturated, edible, spice, herb, germinate, germination, reproduce, reproduction, seasons, life cycle, pollinate, pollination, self-pollinate, cross-pollinate, fertilise, fertilisation, disperse, dispersal, species, minerals, moisture, community, food chains, organism, mini-beast, consumer, producer, decomposer, prey, predator, carnivore, herbivore, omnivore.

RESOURCES

Pictures, charts, photographs, posters of plant life, reference books, CD-Rom, packets of seeds, potting compost, seed trays, pots, thermometer, rulers and measuring tapes, bulbs, beans, fruit and seeds from a range of plants, bedding plants, flowering plants (e.g. buttercup, celery sticks), clear containers, food colouring, sheet of wood/plastic or metal, hand lenses, microscope, collecting nets, containers for mini-beasts, soil trays, the photocopiable sheets *Life cycle of the oak* and *Where is my home?*

NATIONAL CURRICULUM LINKS

Key Stage 2 Science

- Sc 1 Scientific enquiry: 1 Ideas and evidence in science. 2 Investigative skills.
- Sc 2 Life processes and living things: 1 Life processes – pupils should be taught (b) that life processes common to plants include growth, nutrition and reproduction; (c) to make links between life processes in familiar animals and plants and the environment in which they are found. 3 Green plants – pupils should be taught (a) the effect of light, air, water and temperature on plant growth; (b) the role of the leaf in producing new material for growth; (c) that the root anchors the plant and that water and minerals are taken in through the root and transported through the stem to other parts of the plant; (d) about the parts of a flower and their role in the life cycle of flowering plants including pollination, seed formation, seed dispersal and germination. 5 Living things in the environment – pupils should be taught (a) about ways in which living things in the environment need protection; (b) about the different plants and animals found in different habitats; (c) how animals and plants in two different habitats are suited to their environment; (d) to use food chains to show feeding relationships in a habitat; (e) about how nearly all food chains start with a green plant.

ICT suggestions

Word processing for writing up reports of investigations; use of reference material for researching plant life; branch diagrams for classification of plants.

These pictures show the life cycle of the oak tree.
Rearrange them in the correct order and write some
short sentences about each stage.

Find out about the life cycles of other plants.

Find me a home on the oak tree. Can you fit me into a food chain?

10

Margaret Mead

Taking a look at life

People warned her that what she was doing might be dangerous for a single woman, but Margaret Mead knew that the only way to really find out about the people on a small group of remote islands in the Pacific Ocean was to go and live among them.

So in 1925 at the age of twenty-three, having just gained her qualifications at Columbia University and ignoring the advice of her teachers there, she travelled alone to Samoa, where she spent the next two years researching the daily lives of its inhabitants. Her findings were later written up in the best-selling book *Coming of Age in Samoa*. It was the first of forty-four that she wrote about her work and in a long career she also spread her views and beliefs through thousands of articles and hundreds of lectures, talks and interviews all over the world. Because of her strong personality and the fact that she was often outspoken, it was largely through her that anthropology – or the scientific study of people – became such an influential subject.

Margaret Mead was born in Philadelphia in the United States in December 1901. She was one of five children and, although when she was older she aspired to be a painter, her parents convinced her that she should choose science and eventually anthropology. It was not a surprising choice as her mother was a sociologist who specialised in childhood behaviour patterns and her father was an economist. It was her mother who taught Margaret how to observe young children and to make notes on how they acted while she was still a child. She developed this skill when she got to Samoa and careful observation always formed the basis of her work.

In addition to this, Margaret soon realised during her stay in the Pacific that the only real way to get to know a group of people was to learn their language and take an active part in their everyday routines. By doing this and winning their trust she was able to show the people of America that they had much to learn from these so-called 'primitive' islanders. She was particularly impressed with the way that all members of a family, older children, parents, grandparents, aunts, uncles, were involved in helping to rear youngsters. This caused her to believe strongly in the family as a unit and she once said: 'Children are our vehicles for survival, for in them there is hope.'

Margaret studied how youngsters grew and developed through childhood and into adolescence in a culture that had remained essentially unchanged for many generations. She looked at religious beliefs, social relationships especially within families, love and marriage and what affected the decisions people took. Some of her opinions upset people because they challenged the readers' own views about the way children should be reared. Many Americans believed, for example, that the emotional problems suffered by some teenagers were determined by biological factors but Margaret Mead stressed that their behaviour was often more to do with the culture and environment in which they were brought up.

Later on she worked in other parts of the Pacific, including Indonesia, as well as in the United States itself, among American Indians. Her other well-known publications are *Growing Up in New Guinea, Balinese Characters* and her autobiography *Blackberry Winter*. She also wrote and spoke on other important world issues including race relations, drug abuse and population control. Much of her work was carried out for the American Museum of Natural History in New York and at the age of seventy-two she was elected President of the American Association for the Advancement of Science. She died in New York in November 1978 and a year later was posthumously awarded the Presidential Medal of Freedom – the highest civilian honour that can be given to an American citizen.

One of Margaret Mead's greatest abilities was the fact that she could write and speak in such a way that ordinary members of the public were able to understand clearly what she was trying to say. By telling Americans how people lived on the other side of the world, she encouraged them to re-examine their own beliefs and attitudes. In one of her later books she wrote this: 'I have spent most of my life studying the lives of other people so that we can better understand ourselves.' This was, in many ways, her greatest legacy.

THE AGES OF MAN

One of the best ways of getting children to think about their own growth and development is to encourage them to raid the family photograph album. Ask them to bring into school a collection of photographs that chart how they have developed since birth. Three or four pictures are usually enough, showing how they looked soon after birth, as a toddler and when they started school, for example. Discuss the photographs and get children to note down significant changes during the sequence.

- How have they changed facially?
- Is hair colouring different?
- Have there been any alterations in build and stature?
- How has their clothing changed as they have matured?
- Can they pick out friends from their baby photographs?

Statistically minded parents may have kept records of their children's height and weight during their early years and these can be used in conjunction with the photographs. To link with measuring work in mathematics, children should at this stage be able to collect their own personal measurement facts; a record sheet for doing this is provided on the photocopiable sheet *All about me*.

Teachers may be able to persuade a parent or grandparent to come into school to show the children a range of photographs over a longer period of time, even charting what are called the 'seven ages of man'. Many children become fascinated by important facts and figures that are associated with these seven stages. During the foetal period, for example, most of the baby's organs are formed during the first two months. Most infants treble their birth weight during the first year. Newborn babies are reckoned to drink about half a litre of milk each day – about fifteen per cent of their own weight. The heart rate slows gradually from about 150 beats each minute to less than 100 during childhood. Both boys and girls grow fast during adolescence

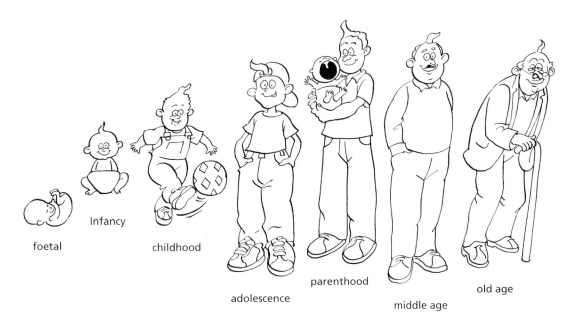

foetal   Infancy   childhood   adolescence   parenthood   middle age   old age

● **Figure 10.1:** The seven ages of man

but girls have the growth spurt earlier than boys because puberty starts earlier for them. Most people have stopped growing by the time they reach parenthood. During pregnancy, a woman gains about twelve kilograms in weight. The sixth stage is called middle age, a time when many people put on weight, the skin can become wrinkly and eyesight problems may develop. Finally, there is old age. Bones become thinner and break more easily and the memory may begin to play tricks. An illustration of these stages in the human life cycle is shown in Figure 10.1. Children may be able to provide their own versions.

Body parts

The human body is both a complex and a fascinating working machine. Children need to know about and understand its basic structure and functions. In addition to more traditional reference materials, there are many excellent models available these days, often life size, of the skeleton and major internal organs that can assist children with their learning. Information can also be found on video and in well-illustrated and colourful big books that are important teaching aids for discussing facts with the whole class.

Start with the skeletal system – the frame of bones that supports the softer parts of the body. An adult has over 200 bones in the body ranging in size from the large thigh bone known as the femur to the tiny stirrup bone in the ear that measures only about three millimetres in length. Talk about the protective role played by bony structures like the skull, the ribs and the backbone. Discuss what bones are made of and what they have running through them. Explain that tough bands called ligaments hold bones together and that muscles enable them to move. Also stress the importance of cartilage, which acts like a lubricated pad at the point where bones need to be able to move smoothly. Children can survey some of the major bones by feeling them on their own bodies. Obvious examples would be the skull, the kneecap, the pelvis, the shinbone, the collarbone and the ribs. It may be possible to acquire some X-rays that will show what a bone looks like when it has been fractured. Then, following further research on the skeleton, ask the children to do their own construction work. Get them initially to build some of the major joints like knees and elbows with cardboard strips and paper fasteners. Once they have gained more experience they should be able to make more refined models with flexible pipe cleaners or art-straws (Figure 10.2). It is also possible to make simplified models of the job carried out by muscles from thick card and elastic bands (Figure 10.3). Facilities may be available for them to test the strength of their muscles with bathroom scales. Push down with each hand in turn to see which is stronger. Then try the fingers individually.

- What readings do they obtain?
- Can they find a suitable way of testing the leg muscles?
- Would they expect one leg to be more powerful than the other one?

Move on to look at the digestive system. This is essentially a tube about ten metres in length that starts at the mouth, ends at the anus and is responsible for breaking up food by mixing it with various chemicals. Children are always surprised to learn that the acid in the stomach is strong enough to burn a hole in thick carpet and that

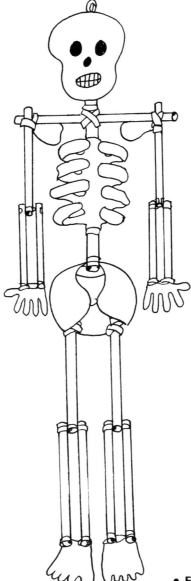

● **Figure 10.2:** Drawing of skeletal model

● **Figure 10.3:** Muscle models

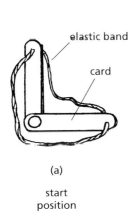

elastic band

card

(a)

start
position

(b)

straight
arm
position

(c)

as one muscle is stretched, its partner is released and vice versa

it takes about thirty hours or more for food to journey right through the system. Using pictures and models, ask the children to piece together in the correct order the various parts of the digestive system and discuss the jobs they carry out. Re-examine the teeth, this time looking at the shape and purpose of the incisors, the canines, the premolars and the molars.

The main purpose of the respiratory system is to take oxygen from the air breathed in and to pass out the waste gas, carbon dioxide. Children will be quick to realise that without air we would not be able to live. Using a tape measure or a piece of string that they can mark themselves, ask them to measure the difference between the chest in the normal position and then after it has been fully expanded during the breathing-in process. Follow this by getting them to observe the rise and fall of the chest as they breathe. See whether they can count the number of breaths taken in one minute. Then ask them to check again after some kind of physical exercise like a run round the playground or climbing up and down a flight of stairs. What changes have occurred? Can they explain why? Try a simple experiment to see how much work the air in the lungs can do. Cut out fish shapes from tissue paper. Blow the fish with one breath. How far does it travel? Some children could breathe out onto a plastic mirror. What has collected on the surface of the mirror? Where has it come from?

A very revealing activity is to provide children with a large silhouette of a human body and ask them to show the locations of the main internal organs. An opportunity to do this is provided on the photocopiable sheet *All about me*. One of the most common errors is the position of the heart, despite its vital role; the kidneys, the liver and the lungs can also cause problems. Many older children will refer to the word 'vein' when talking about the circulation of the blood but few realise that while veins carry blood to the heart it is arteries that take blood away from it. The circulatory system is in many ways like a network of roads in a country. Its main purpose is to transport things around the body including food, warmth, oxygen, waste materials and other chemicals. Check body temperatures before and after exercise. What changes have taken place? Can children explain why this happens? Take pulse rates using the tips of the fingers. What happens to the pulse rate during periods of exercise? How long does it take to return to normal?

Keeping fit

Much has been written about the importance of keeping fit, for both adults and children. But are children aware of how much exercise they need during a typical week and what kind of exercise is best for them?

Over a two-week period, ask the children to record the amount of time they spend exercising, especially out of school hours. They should include activities like walking, swimming, roller-blading, cycling, taking part in competitive sport, as well as areas covered in the physical education curriculum. Chart the results on graphs or using a database. Discuss and classify the different activities into easy, moderate and strenuous, depending on the amount of energy that needs to be put into carrying out the task successfully. Talk about the importance of regular sessions during the two weeks rather than single long bursts. Emphasise that, if exercise is to be really beneficial, it needs to make the cardiovascular system work hard – that is, cause the heart to beat faster and increase the breathing rate. Examine what local leisure facilities are available and how often children use them. Are there gaps in provision? What sorts of costs are involved? How far do they have to travel? Also seek the children's views about methods of relaxation once they have exercised and how, in order to be able to take part in physical activity effectively, they need plenty of sleep.

Encourage the children to develop their own fitness programmes. These activities can be devised and tried during class PE lessons but must also be suitable for outside school hours. Programmes should be arranged to suit the children as individuals. Advice should be given sensitively to avoid embarrassment for children who are conscious about their physical appearance and performance. In this instance it is best to discourage competition and stress the need to work on personal best performances, often referred to as PBs in the world of athletics. Each session needs to start with a warm-up followed by gentle activities before building up to the more strenuous tasks. Also point out that exercise will not only make the heart and lungs work more efficiently but will also improve the body's suppleness, strength and stamina. Children should be encouraged to do the measurement work involved in the fitness programme themselves especially concerning distance and time. Data should be recorded regularly so that progress can be charted over time.

Provide as much variety as possible in the fitness programmes so that children are given the chance to choose the tasks most suitable for them. Include specific exercises for different parts of the body. Some possible suggestions are listed below.

- Timed runs over 40m, 50m, 60m, 80m.
- Timed shuttle relay runs between cones, e.g. $4 \times 10m$ or $2 \times 40m$.
- Sustained running, e.g. half a kilometre.
- Brisk walking over longer distances.
- Obstacle courses involving running and jumping.
- Games involving fetching equipment, set times to beat.
- Sit-ups, press-ups and step-ups, set targets.
- Skipping, set time spans.
- Standing long jumps.
- Throwing a small ball, underarm and over arm, measure the distance.
- Using two hands to throw large ball overhead.
- Swimming and water sport activities, if a pool is available.

SUPPORT

Assist with the personal measurement maths work, especially where reading off scales might become a problem. Advise rounding off units or measuring to the nearest centimetre. Provide plenty of simple models and large, colourful, well-labelled pictures and diagrams to help explain body structure and the functions of vital organs. Help with measuring and cutting out materials when working on body parts like joints and muscles. Set clear goals when children are working on practical tasks associated with breathing and circulation. Help with the structure of fitness programmes and give guidance on collecting and recording times and distances.

EXTENSION

Encourage children to extend the data recorded on personal measurements and work on their ability to collate evidence and draw general conclusions, e.g. common eye colour and average foot size. Stress that background research should be carried out from a wide range of sources, e.g. use of library, checking CD-Roms, etc. Get children to design and make more elaborate body structures and joints combining as many moving parts as possible. Can children devise their own simple tests? Tell them more about the respiratory and circulation systems. See whether children can suggest their own activities to be included in their fitness programmes so that all parts of the body get exercised.

KEY VOCABULARY

Seven ages of human being, life cycle, foetal, infancy, childhood, adolescence, parenthood, middle age, old age, skeleton, internal organs, bones, ligaments, cartilage, muscle, joint, digestive system, oxygen, carbon dioxide, lungs, breathe, breath, heartbeat, kidney, liver, vein, artery, body temperature, pulse rate, exercise, energy, cardiovascular, leisure, relaxation, fitness programme, suppleness, strength, stamina.

RESOURCES

Range of measuring equipment including tape measures, weighing scales, stopwatches and thermometers, models, big books, videos, CD-Roms plus reference materials on body structure and function of major body parts, cardboard, paper fasteners, elastic bands, art-straws, pipe cleaners, scissors, glue, sticky tape, large paper, range of PE equipment for fitness programmes, the

---

NATIONAL CURRICULUM LINKS

Key Stage 2 Science

- Sc 1 Scientific enquiry: 1 Ideas and evidence in science. 2 Investigative skills.
- Sc 2 Life processes and living things: 1 Life processes – pupils should be taught (a) that the life processes common to humans and other animals include nutrition, movement, growth and reproduction. 2 Humans and other animals – Pupils should be taught (c) that the heart acts as a pump to circulate blood through vessels around the body, including through the lungs; (d) about the effect of exercise and rest on the pulse rate; (e) that humans and some other animals have skeletons and muscles to support and protect their bodies and to help them move; (f) about the main stages of the human life cycle; (h) about the importance of exercise for good health.

Key Stage 2 Design and technology

- Developing, planning and communicating ideas.
- Working with tools, equipment, materials and components to make quality products.
- Evaluating processes and products.
- Knowledge and understanding of materials and components.
- Breadth of study: during the key stage pupils should be taught the knowledge, skills and understanding through (c) designing and making assignments using a range of materials.

ICT suggestions

Word processing for reports of investigations; use of reference materials for body parts, functions, etc.; database for recording children's measurements.

• Work with the other members of your group to complete this personal sheet.

My personal record sheet	
First name	
Surname	
Boy/girl	
Age in months	
Height (cm)	
Eye colour	
Hair colour	
Foot length (cm)	
Shoe size	
Pets	

• Set up a database for the computer using the record sheets from the class
• Think of some questions to ask the database

Draw in the position of these bones and organs on the outline of the person

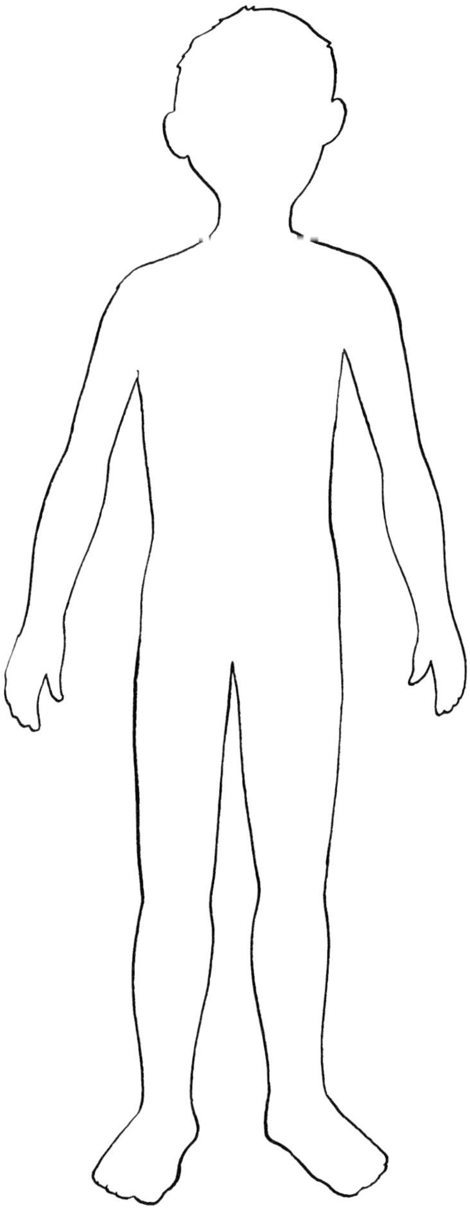

Bones

ribs

pelvis

collarbone

femur

skull

spine

ulna

Organs

heart

lungs

liver

kidney

brain

pancreas

stomach

Index